CIMA Exam Practice Kit

Organisational Management and Information Systems

CIMA Exam Practice Kit

CIMA PUBLISHING

Organisational Management and Information Systems

Darren Sparkes

ELSEVIER

Amsterdam • Boston • Heidelberg • London • New York • Oxford
Paris • San Diego • San Francisco • Singapore • Sydney • Tokyo

CIMA Publishing
An imprint of Elsevier
Linacre House, Jordan Hill, Oxford OX2 8DP
30 Corporate Drive, Burlington, MA 01803

First edition 2008

British Library Cataloguing in Publication Data
A catalogue record for this book is available from the British Library

978 0 7506 8681 5

For information on all CIMA Publishing Publications visit our website at www.cimapublishing.com

Typeset by Integra Software Services Pvt. Ltd, Pondicherry, India
www.integra-india.com

Printed and bound in Hungary

08 09 10 11 12 10 9 8 7 6 5 4 3 2 1

Contents

Learning Outcomes, Syllabus Content and Examination Format

Paper P4 – Organisational Management and Information Systems

Syllabus outline

The syllabus comprises:

Topic and study weighting

- A Information Systems 20%
- B Change Management 10%
- C Operations Management 20%
- D Marketing 20%
- E Managing Human Capital 30%

Learning aims

Students should be able to:

- describe the various functional areas of an organisation and how they relate to one another;
- apply theories, tools and techniques appropriate to a functional area in support of the organisation's strategy;
- prepare reports and plans for functional areas;
- evaluate the performance of functional areas.

Assessment strategy

There will be a written examination paper of 3 hours, with the following sections.

Section A – 40 marks

A variety of compulsory objective test questions, each worth between 2 and 4 marks. Mini-scenarios may be given, to which a group of questions relate.

Section B – 30 marks

Six compulsory short answer questions, each worth 5 marks. A short scenario may be given, to which some or all questions relate.

Section C – 30 marks

One question, from a choice of two, worth 30 marks. Short scenarios may be given, to which all questions relate.

Note: This is a change from the exam paper format used in 2005 and 2006. Section C questions in this kit have been modified to comply with the new assessment strategy.

A – Information Systems – 20%

Learning outcomes

On completion of their studies students should be able to:

1 explain the features and operations of commonly used information technology (IT) hardware and software;
2 explain how commonly used technologies are used in the workplace;
3 identify opportunities for the use of IT in organisations, particularly in the implementation and running of the information system (IS);
4 evaluate, from a managerial perspective, new hardware and software and assess how new systems could benefit the organisation;
5 recommend strategies to minimise the disruption caused by introducing IS technologies;
6 explain how to supervise major IS projects and ensure their smooth implementation;
7 evaluate how IS fits into broader management operations.

Syllabus content

- Introduction to hardware and software in common use in organisations.
- Hardware and applications architectures (i.e. centralised, distributed, client server) and the IT required to run them (PCs, servers, networks and peripherals).
- General Systems Theory and its application to IT (i.e. system definition, system components, system behaviour, system classification, entropy, requisite variety, coupling and decoupling).
- Recording and documenting tools used during the analysis and design of systems (i.e. entity-relationship model, logical data structure, entity life history, dataflow diagram and decision table).
- Databases and database management systems. (*Note*: Knowledge of database structures will not be required.)
- The problems associated with the management of in-house and vendor solutions and how they can be avoided or solved.
- IT-enabled transformation (i.e. the use of information systems to assist in change management).
- System changeover methods (i.e. direct, parallel, pilot and phased).
- IS implementation (i.e. methods of implementation, avoiding problems of non-usage and resistance).
- The benefits of IT systems.
- IS evaluation, including the relationship of subsystems to each other and testing.
- IS outsourcing.
- Maintenance of systems (i.e. corrective, adaptive, preventative).

B – Change Management – 10%

Learning outcomes

On completion of their studies students should be able to:

1 explain the process of organisational development;
2 discuss how and why resistance to change develops within organisations;
3 evaluate various means of introducing change;
4 evaluate change processes within the organisation.

Syllabus content

- External and internal change triggers (e.g. environmental factors, mergers and acquisitions, re-organisation and rationalisation).
- The stages in the change process.
- Approaches to change management (e.g. Beer and Nohria, Kanter, Lewin and Peters, Senge et al.).
- The importance of managing critical periods of change through the life cycle of the firm.

C – Operations Management – 20%

Learning outcomes

On completion of their studies students should be able to:

1 evaluate the management of operations;
2 analyse problems associated with quality in organisations;
3 evaluate contemporary thinking in quality management;
4 explain the linkages between functional areas as an important aspect of quality management;
5 apply tools and concepts of quality management appropriately in an organisation;
6 construct a plan for the implementation of a quality programme;
7 recommend ways to negotiate and manage relationships with suppliers;
8 evaluate a supply network;
9 explain the concept of quality and how the quality of products and services can be assessed, measured and improved.

Syllabus content

- An overview of operations strategy and its importance to the firm.
- Design of products/services and processes and how this relates to operations and supply.
- Methods for managing inventory, including continuous inventory systems (e.g. Economic Order Quantity, EOQ), periodic inventory systems and the ABC system. (*Note*: ABC is not an acronym. A refers to high value, B to medium and C to low value inventory.)
- Strategies for balancing capacity and demand including level capacity, chase and demand management strategies.
- Methods of performance measurement and improvement, particularly the contrast between benchmarking and Business Process Re-engineering (BPR).
- Practices of continuous improvement (e.g. Quality circles, Kaizen, 5S, 6 Sigma).
- The use of benchmarking in quality measurement and improvement.

- Different methods of quality measurement (i.e. operational, financial and customer measures).
- The characteristics of lean production: flexible workforce practices, high-commitment human resource policies and commitment to continuous improvement. Criticisms and limitations of lean production.
- Systems used in operations management: Manufacturing Resource Planning (MRP), Optimised Production Technologies (OPT), Just-in-Time (JIT) and Enterprise Resource Planning (ERP).
- Approaches to quality management, including Total Quality Management (TQM), various British Standard (BS) and European Union (EU) systems as well as statistical methods of quality control.
- External quality standards (e.g. the various ISO standards appropriate to products and organisations).
- Use of the Intranet in information management (e.g. meeting customer support needs).
- Contemporary developments in quality management.
- The role of the supply chain and supply networks in gaining competitive advantage, including the use of sourcing strategies (e.g. single, multiple, delegated and parallel).
- Supply chain management as a strategic process (e.g. Reck and Long's strategic positioning tool, Cousins' strategic supply wheel).
- Developing and maintaining relationships with suppliers.

D – Marketing – 20%

Learning outcomes

On completion of their studies students should be able to:

1 explain the marketing concept;
2 evaluate the marketing processes of an organisation;
3 apply tools within each area of the marketing mix;
4 describe the business contexts within which marketing principles can be applied (consumer marketing, business-to-business (B2B) marketing, services marketing, direct marketing, interactive marketing);
5 evaluate the role of technology in modern marketing;
6 produce a strategic marketing plan for the organisation.

Syllabus content

- Introduction to the marketing concept as a business philosophy.
- An overview of the marketing environment, including societal, economic, technological, physical and legal factors affecting marketing.
- Understanding consumer behaviour, such as factors affecting buying decisions, types of buying behaviour and stages in the buying process.
- Marketing research, including data gathering techniques and methods of analysis.
- Marketing Decision Support Systems (MDSS) and their relationship to market research.
- How business-to-business (B2B) marketing differs from business-to-consumer (B2C) marketing.
- Segmentation and targeting of markets, and positioning of products within markets.
- The differences and similarities in the marketing of products and services.
- Devising and implementing a pricing strategy.
- Marketing communications (i.e. mass, direct, interactive).
- Distribution channels and methods for marketing campaigns.

- The role of marketing in the strategic plan of the organisation.
- Use of the Internet (e.g. in terms of data collection, marketing activity and providing enhanced value to customers and suppliers) and potential drawbacks (e.g. security issues).
- Market forecasting methods for estimating current (e.g. Total Market Potential, Area Market Potential, Industry Sales and Market Shares) and future (e.g. Survey of Buyers' Intentions, Composite of Sales Force Opinions, Expert Opinion, Past-Sales Analysis and Market-Test Method) demand for products and services.
- Internal marketing as the process of training and motivating employees so as to support the firm's external marketing activities.
- Social responsibility in a marketing context.

E – Managing Human Capital – 30%

Learning outcomes

On completion of their studies students should be able to:

1 explain the role of the human resource management (HRM) function and its relationship to other parts of the organisation;
2 produce and explain a HR plan and supporting practices;
3 evaluate the recruitment, selection, induction, appraisal, training and career planning activities of an organisation;
4 evaluate the role of incentives in staff development as well as individual and organisational performance;
5 identify features of a HR plan that vary depending on organisation type and employment model;
6 explain the importance of ethical behaviour in business in general and for the Chartered Management Accountant in particular.

Syllabus content

- The relationship of the employee to other elements of the business plan.
- Determinants and content of a HR plan (e.g. organisational growth rate, skills, training, development, strategy, technologies and natural wastage).
- Problems in implementing an HR plan and ways to manage this.
- The process of recruitment and selection of staff using different recruitment channels (i.e. interviews, assessment centres, intelligence tests, aptitude tests and psychometric tests).
- Issues relating to fair and legal employment practices (e.g. recruitment, dismissal, redundancy and ways of managing these).
- Issues in the design of reward systems (e.g. the role of incentives, the utility of performance-related pay, arrangements for knowledge workers and flexible work arrangements).
- The importance of negotiation during the offer and acceptance of a job.
- The process of induction and its importance.
- Theories of Human Resource Management (e.g. Taylor, Schein, McGregor, Maslow, Herzberg, Handy, Lawrence and Lorsch).
- High performance work arrangements.
- The distinction between development and training, and the tools available to develop and train staff.
- The importance of appraisals, their conduct and their relationship to the reward system.
- HR in different organisational forms (e.g. project-based firms, virtual or networked firms).
- Personal business ethics and the CIMA Ethical Guidelines.

Examination Techniques

Essay questions

Your essay should have a clear structure, that is, an introduction, a middle and an end. Think in terms of 1 mark for each relevant point made.

Report and memorandum

Where you are asked to produce an answer in a report or memorandum format, you will be given easy marks for style and presentation.

- A *report* is a document from an individual or group in one organisation sent to an individual or group in another.
- A *memorandum* is an informal report from one individual or group to another individual or group in the same organisation.

You should start a report or memorandum as follows:

To: J. SMITH, CEO, ABC plc

From: M ACCOUNTANT

Date: 31st December 200X

Terms of Reference: Financial Strategy of ABC plc

1

Information Systems

Information Systems

1

Learning Outcomes

On completion of their studies students should be able to:

- explain the features and operations of commonly used information technology (IT) hardware and software;
- explain how commonly used technologies are used in the workplace;
- identify opportunities for the use of IT in organisations, particularly in the implementation and running of the information system (IS);
- evaluate, from a managerial perspective, new hardware and software and assess how new systems could benefit the organisation;
- recommend strategies to minimise the disruption caused by introducing IS technologies;
- explain how to supervise major IS projects and ensure their smooth implementation;
- evaluate how IS fits into broader management operations.

? Questions

1.1 Within a computer the control unit has three main functions. These are

(i)
(ii)
(iii)

1.2 What is the ALU and what does it do?

1.3 What is the major problem with RAM?

1.4 Identify 3 different input devices and state when you would use them?

1.5 Explain the difference between an operating system, utility programs and communications software.

1.6 Centralised processing means

A All data is processed at a single specialised site
B All data is processed in the centre of the building
C All data entry screens are formatted to be centralised
D All data related to the firms' central heating system is held in one place

1.7 Which of the following statements is true?

A A star network is one that connects all the high fliers in the company
B A ring network is where each member phones the next person on the list
C A tree network is one that has branches everywhere
D A star network is one that has a single server as its hub

1.8 Define each of the following:

(i) Internet
(ii) Intranet
(iii) Extranet

1.9 A DBMS can be defined as:

A A Debenture Marketing Service
B A Debt Measuring System
C A Database Management System
D A Directors Benevolent Service

1.10 What are the four key parts of any system?

(i)
(ii)
(iii)
(iv)

1.11 A feedback control loop is made up of the following components:

(i)
(ii)
(iii)
(iv)

1.12 The purpose of an Invitation to Tender is

A To invite all possible suppliers to a meeting
B To ask the selected supplier to provide a system
C To inform approved suppliers of your requirements
D To request from the customer how much they are prepared to spend

1.13 Name the four symbols used in a data flow diagram:

(i)
(ii)
(iii)
(iv)

1.14 In Entity-Relationship Modelling, which of the following is not a valid relationship?

A One-to-one
B One-to-many
C Many-to-many
D Any-to-some

1.15 Data that is duplicated in more than one file is known as:

A Redundant data
B Outdated data
C Standing data
D Structured data

1.16 The formula for the number of columns in a decision table is

A 2 to the power of n, where n is the number of conditions in the table
B 3 to the power of n, where n is the number of conditions in the table
C 2 to the power of c, where c is the number of consultants employed
D 3 to the power of c, where c is the number of conditions in the decision

1.17 There are 4 tests that must be carried out before a system goes live. These are

(i)
(ii)
(iii)
(iv)

1.18 Changeover to a new system can be achieved by all of the following methods except:

A Parallel running
B Direct changeover
C Phased changeover
D Linear programming

1.19 What are the three forms of maintenance?

(i)
(ii)
(iii)
(iv)

1.20 A light pen can be classified as

A an input device
B an output device
C a storage device
D a processing device

1.21 A digital versatile disk (DVD) can be classified as

A an input device
B an output device
C a storage device
D a processing device

1.22 Linux is an example of

A a utility program
B an application package
C an operating system
D a database management package

1.23 A server is

A a member of the IT department
B an input device
C a shared hardware device
D an application package

1.24 An organisation should be classified as

A a closed system
B a semi-closed system
C an open system
D a financial system

1.25 Information gathering (or fact finding) is a task usually performed during which stage of the systems development life cycle?

A The planning stage
B The analysis stage
C The implementation stage
D The review stage

1.26 In creating a decision table, a question that can only be answered "yes" or "no" is known as

A a decision
B an action
C an open question
D a condition

1.27 A network topology refers to

A the physical arrangement of a computer network
B the type of hardware used
C the hierarchy of access
D the range of software operated

1.28 Entropy is a term used to describe

A the tendency of a system to break down due to randomness
B the tendency of a system to develop over time leading to randomness
C a means of testing candidates in an interview to overcome randomness
D a means of developing open learning using computers

1.29 Data integrity refers to its

A accuracy
B security of storage
C adaptability for multiple use
D ethical use of personal details

1.30 Entity relationship modelling is a technique used within

A an assessment centre test used in staff selection
B market research and product testing
C database analysis and design
D business process re-engineering

1.31 A local area network (LAN) normally contains

A a file, print and communications server(s)
B distributed processing and local solutions
C e-trading and e-marketing
D internet access and firewall protection

1.32 Explain how computer software can assist in achieving quality in a manufacturing organisation.

(4 marks)

1.33 Outline the potential problems of using parallel running during implementation of a new information system.

(4 marks)

1.34 Describe the main benefits of purchasing off-the-shelf software as opposed to in-house developed software.

(4 marks)

1.35 The operating system

A forms part of a system's software
B forms part of a system's hardware
C is another term for a system's hardware
D is a standalone end-user (operator) system solution

1.36 The five elements of a computer system are

A data, communication, flexibility, hardware and data integrit
B installation, hardware, maintenance, audit and compliance
C hardware, software, procedures, data and people
D input, processing, monitoring, control and reporting

1.37 Describe the main advantages of an organisation developing and using an "extranet".

(4 marks)

1.38 Explain the relationship between open systems and adaptive maintenance.

(4 marks)

1.39 Parallel running and pilot schemes are methods of systems changeover. Explain the reasons why an organisation might instead choose a direct approach to a system changeover.

(4 marks)

1.40 Explain the reasons why a department of an organisation might be continuing to use manual records rather than using a new, recently installed and fully operational computer system.

(4 marks)

1.41 A main aim of electronic data interchange (EDI) is

A to improve communication exchanges within an organisation
B to replace conventional documentation with structured electronically transmitted data
C to allow employees to work at home
D to create a shared data resource within an organisation

1.42 "Corrective", "perfective" and "adaptive" are terms associated with

A system maintenance
B change management approaches
C quality assurance
D HR disciplinary processes

✓ Answers

1.1 (i) To read and interpret program instructions.
(ii) To direct the operation of internal processor components.
(iii) To control the flow of programs and data in and out of memory.

1.2 The ALU executes the operations identified by the control unit.

1.3 The major problem with RAM is that it is volatile; when the electrical power is interrupted, data will be lost.

1.4 (i) *Keyboard*: Useful for flexible and variable input by both skilled and unskilled operators. Likely to be used in conjunction with a pointing input tool.
(ii) *Mouse/Trackball/Touchpad*: Point and click devices – useful for navigation and selection purposes. Unlikely to be used on its own, most likely to be used in conjunction with a keyboard.
(iii) *Light pen*: Another point and select tool, but when linked with suitable software they allow plain text input via handwriting recognition software and drawing and design specialisms.

1.5 *The operating system*: This is a set of computer programs that directs the operations of the entire computer system. The most common operating system is Windows.

Utility programs: These are optional add-ons to the operating system, to improve its functions. Common utility programs include anti-virus software and backup utilities.

Communications software: This is primarily designed to support network computer systems or to facilitate email. An example of a common communications package is Microsoft Outlook.

1.6 A

1.7 D

1.8 (i) The *Internet* is a public and global communication network that provides direct connectivity to anyone with a PC and communications connection. Access to it is open to all, which may result in an unruly proliferation of information. Common Internet tools include email, newsgroups, chatting, telephony, electronic conferencing, FTP (file transfer protocol) and Telnet (for remote computer logging in).
(ii) An *Intranet* is an internal organisational network that is based on the Internet technologies, and can be accessed only by authorised employees. While the Internet has open access to the public, an Intranet is private and is protected by a "firewall" (an access control system consisting of hardware and software that is placed between an organisation's internal and external networks).
(iii) An *Extranet* refers to an extended Intranet of an organisation that links to its business partners (e.g. customers, suppliers or other trade organisations). Only authorised users can access to the Extranet. Data transmitted over the Extranet is usually secured. Conceptually, it is not dissimilar from subscription-based Internet sites that require password access.

1.9 C

1.10 (i) Inputs
(ii) Processes
(iii) Outputs
(iv) Environment

1.11 (i) Standard
(ii) Sensor
(iii) Comparator
(iv) Effector

1.12 C

1.13 (i) Data flow
(ii) External entity
(iii) Data store
(iv) Data process

1.14 D

1.15 A

1.16 A

1.17 (i) Realistic tests
(ii) Contrived tests
(iii) Volume tests
(iv) User acceptance tests

1.18 D

1.19 (i) Corrective maintenance
(ii) Perfective maintenance
(iii) Adaptive maintenance

1.20 A

1.21 C

1.22 C

1.23 C

1.24 C

1.25 B

1.26 D

1.27 A

1.28 A

1.29 A

1.30 C

1.31 A

1.32 Software such as computer aided design (CAD) and manufacturing (CAM) provide the necessary flexibility in manufacturing to meet customer requirements more closely and help eliminate mistakes and material wastage. These advances can contribute towards world class manufacturing performance.

1.33 Problems of a parallel changeover include:

- Takes longer - data has to be input twice.
- Increased risk of data input errors as data input twice.
- Increased resource requirements due to duplication of input and running two systems.

- May lead to resistence from employees as they concentrate on using existing system.
- Difficult for management to organise time and resources.

1.34 The main benefits of off-the-shelf software are:

- Speed of supply and installation quicker as readily available and common format for wide ranging compatibility.
- Lower cost as mass produced.
- Lower risk as testing has taken place prior to launch.
- Support offered by vendor for software and product upgrades developed.

1.35 A

1.36 C

1.37 Extranet: an extended Intranet that links business partners.

Advantages:

- Fosters collaboration and information sharing.
- Adds speed and cohesion.
- Facility to link and maximise dispersed networks.
- Enhanced inter-organisational communication.
- Allows electronic data interchange and e-procurement.
- Communication strengthens relationships with customers, suppliers and trade organisations.

1.38 An open system interacts with its external environment. This thinking is consistent with adaptive maintenance. Adaptive maintenance is a mid-to long-term process that adjusts information systems (IS) applications to reflect changing business operations and environments. In this way it accounts for opportunities or threats.

1.39 At a predetermined time an old system ceases entirely and a new one starts. Why this approach?

- Complete confidence in the system.
- Symbolic act to encourage commitment.
- Part of unfreezing the change process.
- Reduced system usage; lower risk of disruption at chosen time.

1.40
- Group resistance to change.
- Cultural resistance.
- Lack of confidence in new system.
- Complexity of new system.
- Efficiency of manual system.
- Individuals' lack confidence to cope.
- Individuals' jobs feel threatened.
- Ineffective management, control, communication, training, support and so on.

1.41 B

1.42 A

? Section B question

Question 1

X is a large financial services company. It employs over 500 staff, and sells a full range of savings and loan products through a large call centre.

A customer seeking, for example, a loan to buy a new car would call the X call centre and speak to a telesales operator. The operator would ask the customer a series of questions about the customer's income, lifestyle and proposed car purchase. The operator is prompted with each question by a sophisticated computerised "expert system", designed by X's IT department. The customer's answer to each question is input into the expert system. When all the required information has been input, the system decides whether or not the customer should receive the loan and, if so, what interest rate will be charged. If a customer's loan application is approved, the customer is sent a paper application form for signature and return. The customer must also provide three forms of identification, such as a birth certificate, driving licence, identity card or electricity bill. Once all the required information has been received, the customer is sent a cheque for the loan amount.

Requirements

(a) Identify five input or output devices that X might use to support the call centre operations

(5 marks)

(b) Explain what is meant by "backup", explaining its relevance to the operations of X

(5 marks)

(c) Identify three application packages (other than the expert system described) that X might use, explaining their relevance to the operations of X.

(5 marks)

(d) Explain what is meant by client-server computing, and explain to X how it might be used in their business.

(5 marks)

(e) Describe what is meant by email and explain the advantages, to X, of using it in their business.

(5 marks)

(f) Explain what is meant by a decision table, and identify one aspect of X's business where this technique may be of value.

(5 marks)
(Total = 30 marks)

Section B question

Answer 1

(a) Five input or output devices that X might use are as follows:

1 Input device – keyboard. The operator will need to enter the customer's answers to the expert system.
2 Input device – mouse. The operator will need to select from the different input areas on the screen.
3 Output device – screen. The operator will need to see the questions and input areas for answers.
4 Output device – printer. The application form will need printing before it is sent to the customer.
5 Input device – scanner. The customer's documents can be scanned into the system, to eliminate the need to store copies.

(b) Backup is the process of storing copies of software and data so that it can be recovered in the event of a system failure. Backups of software are normally made onto CD-ROM or DVD, and stored in a safe place. Data backups should be made as often as data changes, normally onto DVD or tape, and stored in a fireproof safe. X should backup all of their operating systems and application software, including the expert system. These backups should be updated every time the systems change. Data should be backed up regularly, throughout the day, as it changes frequently.

(c) Three application packages that X might use are as follows;

1 Word processing – this could be used for the production of correspondence, such as the application form sent to customers.
2 Email – this could be used to get additional information from customers. It would be faster than relying on the post, and customers could attach copies of identification documents.
3 Accounting – this would allow X to keep track of loans, savings products and customer transactions.

(d) Client-server computing refers to the division of operations in a computer network between end-users (clients) and the processors that provide services to them (servers). A client is any PC or workstation connected to the network. In X, each of the operators, and any support staff, would have access to a client workstation. A server is any networked computer that provides a specific service such as managing files, controlling communications or performing applications. In X, a server would run the expert system, as this is a shared application.

(e) Electronic mail (or email) systems are designed to allow electronic communication between individuals in different locations. Email systems use either private networks or, more commonly, the Internet. The benefits of email to X would be as follows:

1 Speed – email allows almost instant communication, so X could process applications faster.
2 Versatility – email allows file attachments, so customers could scan and send identification documents to X.
3 Evidence – email systems keep copies of correspondence, so an audit trail can be seen. This is important for X as it deals with money.

(f) Decision tables are used to describe the processing logic of a system. The most useful application of decision tables is where there may be a number of different conditions to evaluate. An example of such a system is the expert system used by X, which could be modelled using a decision table. Conditions could include income levels and home ownership, and actions could include rejecting the loan or granting it at different interest rates. X could use decision tables during any systems analysis or redesign exercise.

? Section C question

Question 1

S is a manufacturing company which produces DVD players and other electronic consumer products. It is structured along conventional functional lines with departments of production, purchasing, finance, marketing and sales, research and development and packaging.

In recent years, it has faced an increasingly changing and unpredictable environment; as competition from overseas rivals has increased, late delivery of some components has led to production delays and new legislation has pushed up employee insurance and pension costs.

The introduction of new technology to try to improve efficiency in production has met with limited success as employees have found the new work processes excessively boring. This has led in turn to demands from the workforce for an increase in pay. Attempts to improve performance have not been helped by the constant battles between the head of production and the head of marketing over the design of some key products.

Requirements

(a) Explain the open systems approach to organisational analysis.

(12 marks)

(b) Explain how "S" could apply the open systems approach to identify areas for improving its efficiency and competitiveness.

(18 marks)
(Total = 30 marks)

Section C question

Answer 1

(a) The basic idea of the open systems approach is that organisations possess mechanisms which take inputs from the environment and subject these inputs to various transformation processes that result in outputs. The term "open" in this context is used to make clear that the boundaries of the organisation are open to accept inputs of various kinds, be this information or other resources.

> **Examiner's Note:**
> A variety of models have been devised to illustrate the open systems approach. Any of these are acceptable inclusion, provided they contain the basic features described within this answer.

The open nature of the organisation as a system also implies that any change in the organisation's environment, whether this is in the broader macroenvironment or its more immediate industry environment, will have an impact on the organisation's operations.

Furthermore, organisations are seen as being composed of interdependent parts, so that any changes that occur in one part of the organisational system will result in changes in other parts of the organisation.

The parts that make up the organisation as a system can be conceptualised in a variety of ways. One common description is in terms of a number of subsystems such as task, technology, structure, people and management.

For example, one influential study of the coal-mining industry in the 1940s by Trist and Bamforth demonstrated the close links between the social and psychological needs of employees and the technical requirements of coal production. The introduction of new coal-cutting machinery was accompanied by the break-up of close-knit teams of miners. The outcome of this new arrangement was a decline in morale and productivity among the miners. Only when a new form of team working was restored to "fit" with the requirements of the new technology, were morale and productivity restored to former levels. This and later studies established what Trist and Bamforth came to call the "socio-technical systems approach". This involves management in seeking to ensure that the needs of employees are taken into account whenever new technology is introduced so that the "technical" subsystem and the "social" subsystem are compatible.

But equally well, the subsystems might be regarded as functional departments that go to make up an organisation as a system, as in the scenario example. The important point is that organisations can be regarded as made up of many different parts that can be regarded as subsystems and that these parts must fit together in certain ways to ensure the optimum working of the whole organisation.

Finally, as open systems, organisations need to maintain favourable transactions of inputs and outputs with the environment in order to survive over time and this necessarily involves the organisation's management retaining favourable relationships with key stakeholders such as customers, suppliers, government and the wider community.

(b) Having outlined the nature of the organisation as an open system, we can now consider how this perspective can assist in the identification of areas for improvements in the competitiveness of a manufacturing organisation like the S Company.

Given the assumptions of the open systems approach, attention is directed to the relationships between the Company and its environment and to the relationships between the various parts and processes of the organisation.

The number of potential problems posed by the environment is considerable as threats may come not only from the competition as indicated in the brief scenario, but also from a range of relationships with other aspects of the macro-environment including the economic, political, social or technological and from those within the industry such as potential new entrants, suppliers, buyers and other external stakeholders.

In the case of the S Company, the threat has come from overseas competitors, from suppliers and from government legislation but the open systems perspective alerts the S Company to continually monitor other aspects of the environment for potential threats and for opportunities.

If we define the various functional departments as subsystems, then it follows that while the threat of overseas competition has implications for the S Company as a whole, the problem with suppliers has particular implications for the purchasing subsystem. The purchasing department, in particular, will have to respond to the threat by seeking alternative means of supply or some other way of dealing with the threat. New legislation on pensions and insurance will push up costs for the whole organisation but particular subsystems such as those that deal with human resources and finance will be most directly affected and thus expected to respond. This may mean tighter budgets for labour and a consequent slimming down of the workforce.

The open systems perspective also directs attention to the interdependent relationships between the various parts and processes within the organisation. In the case of the S Company, inefficiencies may lie in the nature of relationships between the functional departments. For example, there may be production delays because purchasing has failed to ensure supplies at the right time or in the right quantity.

The reference in the scenario to the conflict between subsystems of production and marketing can also be regarded as an example of the kind of dysfunctional relationship that an open systems approach would call attention to.

Alternatively, there may be a lack of "fit" between the "social" and "technical" subsystems because insufficient attention has been given to aligning the requirements of employees for a humane working environment with the requirements of the new technology. This is suggested by the fact that employees find the new system to be boring and possibly by their demand for more pay which may be a symptom of their dissatisfaction with the new system of work.

In fact, there may be problems caused by poor co-ordination between any of the subsystems, within the S Company that need to be improved in order to promote greater efficiency within the organisation.

2

Operations Management and Quality

Operations Management and Quality

2

Learning Outcomes

On completion of their studies students should be able to:

- evaluate the management of operations;
- analyse problems associated with quality in organisations;
- evaluate contemporary thinking in quality management;
- explain the linkages between functional areas as an important aspect of quality management;
- apply tools and concepts of quality management appropriately in an organisation;
- construct a plan for the implementation of a quality programme;
- recommend ways to negotiate and manage relationships with suppliers;
- evaluate a supply network;
- explain the concept of quality and how the quality of products *and* services can be assessed, measured and improved.

? Questions

2.1 Mintzberg described organisations in terms of all of the following except:

A Technostructure
B Infrastructure
C Strategic apex
D Middle line

2.2 Porter stated that the value chain had four secondary activities. These included all of the following except:

A Technology development
B Procurement
C Support staff
D Human resource management

2.3 Reck and Long's positioning tool described approaches to purchasing. It included all of the following except:

A Passive
B Interactive
C Independent
D Integrative

2.4 The four main sourcing options for an organisation are

(i)
(ii)
(iii)
(iv)

2.5 The benefits of Manufacturing Resource Planning (MRPII) include all of the following except:

A Reduced stockholding
B Increased customer service
C Slower deliveries
D Improved facilities utilisation

2.6 Define Total Productive Maintenance (TPM).

2.7 Quality can be defined as:

A Fitness for purpose
B Highest possible standard
C Highest standard at acceptable cost
D Something that exceeds customer specifications

2.8 TQM stands for:

A Targeted Quality Measurement
B Total Quality Measurement
C Targeted Quality Management
D Total Quality Management

2.9 Ouchi's "Theory Z" stated that all of the following principles were important except:

A Emphasis on dictatorial management approaches
B Emphasis on interpersonal skills
C Emphasis on participative management
D Emphasise on informal and democratic relationships

2.10 Who popularised the phrase "Zero Defects"?

A Edward Deming
B Joseph Juran
C Philip Crosby
D Kuaro Ishikawa

2.11 The four Cs of Quality are

(i)
(ii)
(iii)
(iv)

2.12 What is the difference between Quality Control (QC) and Quality Assurance (QA)?

2.13 Name the four types of costs associated with quality.

(i)
(ii)
(iii)
(iv)

2.14 Define Quality Circles.

2.15 There are three different types of benchmarking. These are all of the following except:

A Internal
B Competitor
C Best practice
D Total quality

2.16 Define Business Process Re-engineering (BPR).

2.17 Name the five processes or phases in BPR:

(i)
(ii)
(iii)
(iv)
(v)

2.18 Define Innovation and explain what it attempts to do.

2.19 What are the six criteria in Brown et al.'s test for "enlightened" organisations wishing to measure performance?

(i)
(ii)
(iii)
(iv)
(v)
(vi)

2.20 According to Mintzberg, which of the following is NOT one of the components of organisational structure?

A Middle line
B Operating core
C Oligarchy
D Technostructure

2.21 In the value chain, which of the following is a "secondary" or "support" activity?

A Procurement
B Service
C Marketing and sales
D Operations

2.22 According to Cousins, which of the following is a "spoke" of the "supply wheel"?

A Procurement
B Operations
C Cost/benefit analysis
D Sales

2.23 According to Porter, a collection of related value chains is known as

A an industry
B a value system
C a market
D a barrier to entry

2.24 If ABC is NOT "Activity Based Costing", then it is

A a supplier management approach
B a way of selecting operations staff
C a way of teaching procurement staff
D an inventory management classification

2.25 JIT is

A A "push" system
B A "pull" system
C A "closed" system
D A "feedback" system

2.26 The "M" in "TPM" stands for

A Manufacturing
B Management
C Maintenance
D Marketing

2.27 According to Ouchi, "Theory Z" is a compromise between

A Theory X and Theory Y
B Theory A and Theory J
C Theory A and Theory B
D Theory Y and Theory J

2.28 ISO 14001 is a quality standard for

A total quality
B environmental quality
C investment in people
D corporate governance

2.29 The 5-S framework is used as

A a checklist for quality control
B a set of controls for maintenance
C a tool to improve the management of operations
D a TQM tool

2.30 Attempting to influence demand by smoothing variations above or below capacity is known as which of the following capacity management strategies:

A Chase demand
B Demand management
C Level capacity
D Mixed approach

2.31 Explain the main features of a (Just-in-Time) JIT system.

(4 marks)

2.32 Identify four common reasons for the failure of TQM programmes

(4 marks)

2.33 Core features of world-class manufacturing involve

A competitor benchmarking and an investment in training and development
B an investment in IT and technical skills
C global sourcing networks and an awareness of competitor strategies
D a strong customer focus and flexibility to meet customer requirements

2.34 Corrective work, the cost of scrap and materials lost are

A examples of internal failure costs
B examples of external failure costs
C examples of appraisal costs
D examples of preventative costs

2.35 Reck and Long's strategic positioning tool identifies an organisation's

A purchasing approach
B sales approach
C manufacturing approach
D warehousing approach

2.36 Inbound logistics is

A a secondary activity that refers to price negotiation of incoming raw materials
B a secondary activity that refers to receipt, storage and inward distribution of raw materials
C a primary activity that refers to inbound enquiries and customer complaints
D a primary activity that refers to receipt, storage and inward distribution of raw materials

2.37 Supply chain partnerships grow out of

A quality accreditation
B recognising the supply chain and linkages in a value system
C an expansion of trade
D adopting a marketing philosophy

2.38 International standard ISO 14001 "Environmental Management Systems" encourages processes for controlling and improving an organisation's

A performance on "green" issues
B performance on quality issues as they relate to the competitive environment
C performance on scanning an industry environment
D performance on its internal investment in people

Answers

2.1 B

2.2 C

2.3 B

2.4 (i) Single
(ii) Multiple
(iii) Delegated
(iv) Parallel

2.5 C

2.6 Total Productive Maintenance (TPM) is a contemporary idea aimed at increasing the productivity of the organisation's equipment. The fundamental objective of TPM is to prevent quality failures caused by equipment failure or degradation so TPM might usefully contribute a quality management programme. It involves identifying equipment in every division, including planning, manufacturing and maintenance, and then planning and implementing a maintenance programme that covers their entire useful life.

2.7 A

2.8 D

2.9 A

2.10 C

2.11 (i) Commitment
(ii) Competence
(iii) Communication
(iv) Continuous improvement

2.12 Quality Assurance attempts to create quality whilst Quality Control merely attempts to control an existing agreed level of quality. QC deals with validating an existing standard. QA seeks to innovate and improve.

2.13 (i) Prevention Costs
(ii) Appraisal Costs
(iii) Internal Failure Costs
(iv) External Failure Costs

2.14 A Quality Circle is a multidisciplinary group of staff whose brief is to identify, investigate and solve work-related problems. The concept of a circle is important for two reasons:

(i) The concept of a circle never ends, hence the constant search for improvement.
(ii) Within a quality circle there is no hierarchy. Rather like the Arthurian round table, all players are equal.

2.15 D

2.16 The fundamental rethinking and radical redesign of business processes to achieve dramatic improvements in critical, contemporary measures of performance, such as cost, quality, service and speed (Hammer and Champy, 2001).

2.17 (i) Planning
(ii) Internal learning
(iii) External learning
(iv) Redesign
(v) Implementation

2.18 Innovation is the introduction of new and improved ways of doing things at work. Innovation involves deliberate attempts to bring about benefits from new changes; these include increases in productivity and improvements in the design and quality of products. Innovations may include technological changes such as new products, but may also include new production processes, the introduction of advanced manufacturing technology or the introduction of new computer support services within an organisation.

2.19 (i) Relevant
(ii) Integrated
(iii) Balanced
(iv) Strategic
(v) Improvement-orientated
(vi) Dynamic

2.20 C

2.21 A

2.22 C

2.23 B

2.24 D

2.25 B

2.26 C

2.27 B

2.28 B

2.29 C

2.30 B

2.31 The main features of a Just-in-Time (JIT) systems are:

- Pulls work through the system in response to demand.
- Operates with minimum inventory levels.
- Strong relationships with suppliers to ensure quality.
- Development of a responsible and flexible workforce.
- Elimination of non-value-added activities.
- An emphasis on continuous improvement and the pursuit of excellence.

2.32 Four common reasons for the failure of TQM programmes are:

- Tail off – After an initial burst of enthusiasm top management fails to maintain interest and support.
- Deflection – Other initiatives or problems deflect attention away from TQM.

- Lack of buy-in – Management pays only lip service to the principle of worker involvement and open communication.
- Rejection – TQM is not compatible with the organizations' wider culture and ways of doing things.

2.33 D

2.34 A

2.35 A

2.36 D

2.37 B

2.38 A

? Section B questions

Question 1

You are a researcher employed by a topical business discussion television show "Round The Table". Next week's discussion is about managing supply to achieve quality and customer satisfaction. Invited guests will be a leading academic, public and private sector senior managers and the chief executive of a car producer. You have been asked to prepare an outline briefing that will give some background information to the show's presenter.

Your research shows that the automobile industry is highly competitive and globally suffers from "overcapacity". In certain countries however, there is unfulfilled demand for specialist makes and models, implying some under capacity "hot spots". You understand that for any organisation, whether producing goods or services, effective capacity management is vital. It ensures that customers' needs are more fully met and that there are fewer unfulfilled delivery date promises. There are several ways of dealing with variations in demand and matching production capacity including:

- concentrating on inventory levels (a "Level capacity" strategy).
- concentrating on demand (a "Demand" strategy).
- adjusting levels of activity (a "Chase" strategy).

As part of your investigation you note that distinctive issues exist for service organisations (such as those found in the public sector) compared with manufacturing organisations (such as car producers).

Requirements

As the show's researcher you are required to produce guidance notes to support the show's presenter which:

(a) discuss why a level capacity strategy might be difficult for a firm wishing to adopt a just-in-time (JIT) philosophy;

(5 marks)

(b) discuss the impact of demand strategies on an organisation's marketing practices;

(5 marks)

(c) discuss the relationship between chase strategies and the flexible organisation;

(5 marks)

(d) identify the ways that service organisations differ from manufacturing organisations when considering capacity management;

(5 marks)

(e) describe the types of software applications a manufacturing firm might introduce to improve its inbound logistics;

(5 marks)

(f) describe the types of computerised assistance that could be used by those involved in selling cars and wanting to improve demand.

(5 marks)

Notes (a) to (d) should have particular regard to quality, capacity and other organisational issues.

(Total = 30 marks)

✓ Section B questions

Answer 1

Requirement (a)

Level Capacity Strategy: difficult for a firm wishing to adopt a JIT philosophy.

About level capacity
Level capacity involves building inventory levels to deal with increases in demand beyond "normal". This suggests a building of buffer stocks of (for instance) cars to deal with excess demand. The notion of buffer stocks is wholly inconsistent with a firm wishing to adopt a quality drive just-in-time (JIT) philosophy.

About JIT
JIT is considered key to many organisational quality programmes. JIT production methods involve each component on a production line being produced only when it is needed and not before. An outcome of JIT is an elimination of large stocks of materials and parts not a building of them (as level capacity strategies imply).

Key Points

- Customer satisfaction may be improved short term by adopting a level capacity strategy (making immediate delivery possible). However, these "buffer" stocks are inconsistent with the JIT quality approach.
- Level capacity increases stockholding costs and may not be the most cost-effective means of capacity management.
- Organisational requirement: more working capital to build stocks.
- A more lasting means of achieving customer satisfaction might be the full adoption of a quality philosophy instead.

Requirement (b)

The impact of demand strategies on an organisation's marketing practices.

About demand strategies
Demand strategies attempt to influence demand to "smooth" variations so that the organisation is better able to cope. This represents a type of manipulation and influence over demand so that it is "made" to "fit" supply capability.

About marketing
The marketing function will want to ensure that the marketing mix (Product/service, Price, Promotion and Place) is appropriate for the individual organisation and may:

- Vary price to encourage/slow down demand
- Intensify promotion in "slack" periods
- Restrict sales outlets (place) when there is excess demand.

Marketing practice can, in ways such as these, support demand strategies.

Key Points

- The marketing tactics above represent short-term practices and may not benefit the firm long term. It might, for instance, lead to reduced satisfaction when customers are frustrated by the restrictions of place. They may indeed decide to switch to a competitor's product.

- The use of demand strategies in conjunction with marketing practice suggests that the organisation is not marketing orientated. The main focus is not the customer, rather, it is internal production considerations. This philosophy will ultimately hurt quality, which has the customer as central.
- In terms of organisational implications, profitability may be affected as a result of financing sales promotions and price reductions.

Requirement (c)

About chase strategies

Chase strategies involve constantly adjusting activity levels to shadow fluctuations in demand. This demonstrates market responsiveness and closeness to customer demands.

About flexible organisations

There is something of an organisational trend emerging that has "non traditional" organisational structures and a flexible workforce. These measures allow organisations to display maximum flexibility and responsiveness to customer demands. By using a flexible organisation approach to accommodate "peaks and troughs", chase strategies will be possible, specifically:

- Organisational structures may achieve operational flexibility by becoming less rigid in terms of hierarchy.
- Skills flexibility might be achieved by cross training employees to perform different operations. Integration of tasks can occur both horizontally (undertaking a broader range of tasks at the same level as their original task) and vertically (undertaking tasks previously carried out by employees at other levels).
- Atkinson's worker categories involve core and periphery staff (temporary/part-time) to act as a buffer against changes in demand. Numerical flexibility might be achieved by an increased use of temporary, part-time, short-term contract working and outsourcing work at peak times. Such flexibility might be achieved by using both contractors and agency staff.

Key Points

- The two concepts complement one another.
- Such an approach would more easily achieve customer satisfaction.
- It would be consistent with a quality ethos, as flexible manufacturing is at the heart of a quality approach.
- Organisational implications include structures, HR policies and practice, rewards, recruitment and training. Organisationally, there should also be a commitment to continuous improvement, including the use of quality circles.

Requirement (d)

Capacity Management: the ways that service organisations differ from manufacturing organisations.

Differences for a service organisation

- The consumer is a participant in the service process (unlike the purchaser of a manufactured good).
- The characteristics of the workforce determines the effectiveness of the service to a greater degree, as the consumer/worker interaction is central.
- Services are perishable.

- Services are intangible, so communication is more difficult when explaining the benefits of a purchase. This makes marketing more complex.
- Output measurement is less easy to evidence. (Outputs for Not-for-Profit (NFP) organisations are often multiple).
- NFP funding may be government determined and may be insufficient to finance all customer demands immediately, which implies a need for a rationing of service.
- For NFP organisations, consumers may be a different grouping from those paying for the service to be provided. This is confusing when concentrating on customers, as there are multiple customers to satisfy, each with different, sometimes contradictory, demands.

Key Points

- The level capacity strategy assumes that units of production are durable and can be stored (as is the case with cars). This may not be possible for perishable goods and services more generally. (It is impossible to "stockpile" consultancy advice.)
- There may be a lack of customer satisfaction if (using a medical treatment example), waiting lists appear.
- Quality issues are more overtly of a human kind as the workforce determines the quality of the service.
- Organisational implications include appropriate HR policies to ensure that employees deal with customers appropriately and impact positively on customer satisfaction levels. Good systems to support delivery of the services are also important.

Requirement (e)

The types of software applications a manufacturing firm might introduce to improve inbound logistics.

This can be understood in the context of Michael Porter's value chain model, as follows:

- Inbound logistics: one of five primary activities directly concerned with the creation or delivery of a product.
- Support activities: help improve the efficiency and effectiveness of primary activities and include technology development (and therefore, software applications).

The issue becomes the *types* of software applications that would help with inbound logistics, including receiving, storing and distributing materials (material handling, stock control and transport, and so on). These applications may be developed in-house or purchased as off the shelf.

Types of applications include:

- Software that assists inventory management (whether method used is continuous, periodic inventory or ABC, and so on).
- Warehousing, including storage and re-ordering. (Under a just-in-time system, the matching of the receipt of material closely with usage is key to reducing stockholding levels and costs. Larger organisations would certainly need IT support. Software is capable of producing reports to ensure that quantities held in stock are within the predetermined budgets).
- Software capable of assisting the management of transport including work scheduling.
- Benchmarking database of inbound activities. This allows a convenient and systematic comparison to be made of practice and/or process with suitable comparator organisations and other sections.
- Internet enabled purchasing software from suppliers possible using an E-catalogue.
- Software to assist purchasing, possibly databases of suppliers where issues of quality and price can be monitored.

One specific example of software:

- Manufacturing Resource Planning (MRP) (for example MRP II), a system that assists capacity management through a matching supply and demand. Organisational implications: Reduced stock holding and stock turnover, and improved facilities usage. Customer satisfaction: Fewer delays through materials shortage, certainty over delivery times.

Requirement (f)

Selling cars and wanting to improve demand: the types of computerised assistance that could be used.

Cars are consumer goods and sales and promotion strategies are important to both car manufacturer and dealers. Sales and promotion strategies (along with the other Ps including price) will help determine demand.

Computerised technology might be used in a number of ways in order to communicate with existing, past and potential customers the benefits of the products (car models) and so stimulate demand.

Examples include:

- *Database of potential customers* may be good for targeting particular customers and their likely requirements. It enables messages to be personalised. This allows for direct letter mailing of promotional literature. It is also easier to improve customer relationships and hence buyer loyalties by customer follow-up contact after sales are made. In terms of customer satisfaction, it might be viewed either positively or negatively as "junk mail".
- *Advertising using the internet* to a less targeted audience. A non-personal presentation using email technology and site "pop-ups". In terms of customer satisfaction it might be viewed negatively as "SPAM" mail and a nuisance. Alternatively, it might reinforce a positive message.
- *Engaging in E-Business*. A dealer could potentially supplement or replace an existing showroom site by developing electronically based systems and technologies of doing business. Savings made on premises costs could be passed on to customers, so enhancing their satisfaction.
- *Technology supported market research* could help provide in-depth analysis of a single market so enabling informed decisions to be made aimed at improving demand. Technology supported market research might form a sub-system feeding a more comprehensive marketing database and Management Information System (MIS). MIS might include comparative competitor approaches to stimulating demand.
- *Vehicle dashboard displays*. Cars could be fitted with microchips that indicate when a vehicle is in need of a service (for example after 20,000 miles). Alternative examples include a display of dealer contact details when a vehicle is in need of replacement (for example after 3 years), and so on

? Section C questions

Question 1

The O Company, founded in the 1960s, manufactures electric pumps. Despite developments in globalisation, technology, methods of production, techniques of quality management and global sourcing of supplies, the O Company has retained its original approach to operations.

Unfortunately, this reluctance to adapt to the new operations environment has resulted in a decline in competitiveness, a consequent fall in market share, and an overall threat to the future viability of the O Company.

Requirements

(a) Describe the key activities in the operations function of an organisation such as the O Company.

(10 marks)

(b) Explain how the O Company could take advantage of the opportunities offered by developments in technology, production methods, quality management and global sourcing to improve its competitiveness.

(20 marks)
(Total = 30 marks)

Section C questions

Answer 1

(a) The operations function is concerned with the conversion of resource inputs into outputs of goods and services. Operations cover a wide range of activities including purchasing, production, distribution and logistics. The term "operations" has traditionally been associated with the manufacture of products but with the increasing importance of the service sector, the operations function is recognised as a vital function in this sector also.

In the case of a manufacturing company like the O Company, operations include the following activities:

Purchasing involves the sourcing and buying of raw materials, components and the tools and equipment necessary for the manufacture of electric pumps.

Production involves the conversion of raw materials and the assembly of components into finished items. In the case of the O Company, production might encompass the actual making of components as well as the assembly of bought-in components. For example, the O Company might cast some parts of its electric pumps in its foundry or it may produce some of the components by turning them on a lathe.

Production in the O Company will probably be the form of mass production rather than job, or batch production.

Associated with the conversion process of production are the various *control mechanisms* to ensure control of output and quality. In the case of the O Company, this would include some kind of production scheduling and some form of quality assurance.

Once the assembled electric pumps are ready to leave the factory, *logistical considerations* will become important. These will involve such things as where to hold the finished product, in what quantity and with what delivery schedule to customers.

Transport can also be considered part of operations and will include considerations to do with economic delivery quantity and mode of transport to be used.

Distribution will be concerned with whether to distribute the electric pumps directly to customers or through wholesalers and retailers.

(b) The more important developments in technology since the 1960s include the development of the microchip. This has enabled the development of computers, the Internet and information technology in general. It has enabled the development of computer-controlled machines and thus impacted on manufacturing methods.

As far as the production of electric pumps in the O Company is concerned, these developments open up the possibility of greater productivity and hence lower costs.

In the production area, computer-controlled machines allow for greater flexibility in the making of parts or different models of pumps. The saving here comes from reduced time in the setting up of machines.

The development of the Internet and Intranets also enhance the speed and reduce the cost of both external and internal communications and provide more efficient storage of data and access to that data.

Since the 1960s, there have also been developments in how goods like electric pumps are produced. Developments in electronics have in turn aided the automation of production in some areas via the development of robotics. These "intelligent" machines are faster, more precise and more consistent than humans and so have replaced some of the simpler more repetitive tasks previously carried out by manual labour. Not only are these machines more efficient but they have improved quality by virtue of their capacity to maintain consistent standards.

Some of the most important changes in the methods of production have been developed by Japanese companies and have since been copied worldwide. These methods include Just-in-Time (JIT) delivery and production. JIT involves a production system which is driven by demand for finished products, whereby each component on a production line is produced only when needed for the next stage. Similarly, the delivery of parts for production or assembly arrives JIT for production to take place. In an electric pump manufacturing business like the O Company, the savings will derive from the saving in inventory. The Company will be saved the expense of storage of components at the input end of the production process and of assembled electric pumps at the output end of the process.

Developments in quality assurance, also developed by the Japanese, can improve the product quality of the O Company's electric pumps. Japanese companies have used total quality management (TQM) to great effect in improving the quality of their products. In order to reap similar benefits, the O Company needs to adopt TQM. This will involve adherence to the following principles – recognition of the importance of the customer, the need for employees in all functions to be involved in quality improvement and the adoption of the principle of continuous improvement. In order to put these principles into practice, there will be a need to invest in employee training and development, an encouragement to develop team working and especially cross-functional teams and the involvement of customers and suppliers in the process.

The improvements in transportation and communications have made the global sourcing of many materials and components a distinct possibility and thus reduce the costs of inputs to the production process. Just which materials and components the O Company might source from other countries is impossible to say without comparative cost information, but high value, low-weight components will be high on its list of priorities.

3

Marketing

Marketing

3

Learning Outcomes

Marketing accounts for 20% of the overall syllabus. The chapter introduces marketing as an important topic, and will help enable you to:

- explain the marketing concept;
- evaluate the marketing processes of an organisation;
- apply tools within each area of the marketing mix;
- describe the business contexts within which marketing principles can be applied;
- evaluate the role of technology in modern marketing;
- produce a strategic marketing plan for the organisation.

? Questions

3.1 Marketing has been defined as:

A The management process responsible for advertising.
B The management process responsible for getting people to buy products they do not want.
C The management process responsible for identifying, anticipating and satisfying customer requirements, profitably.
D The management process responsible for dealing with customer complaints.

3.2 Name the four organisational philosophies:

(i)
(ii)
(iii)
(iv)

3.3 The four Ps of the Marketing Mix are

(i)
(ii)
(iii)
(iv)

3.4 The PLC stands for:

A The Product Liability Chart
B The Product's Limited Character
C The Product Life Cycle
D The Product Life Chart

3.5 What does B2B mean and why is this an important concept?

3.6 Questions that would be addressed under "Place" in the marketing mix include all of the following except:

A Where will the customer use the product?
B Is the means of distribution appropriate?
C Is the product available in the right quantities?
D Is the place of purchase convenient to the customer?

3.7 Describe the difference between a "pull" and a "push" promotional campaign.

3.8 Identify the three perspectives on pricing proposed by Lancaster and Withey.

(i)
(ii)
(iii)

3.9 The extended marketing mix includes a further 3 Ps. These include all of the following except:

A People
B Physical evidence
C Process
D Procedures

3.10 What does B2C mean and why is this an important concept?

3.11 Define Market Segmentation.

3.12 Kotler's three criteria for segmentation include all of the following except:

A Measurable
B Accessible
C Homogenous
D Substantial

3.13 What does FMCG mean?

3.14 List the five stages in a consumer decision process, according to Lancaster and Withey.

(i)
(ii)
(iii)
(iv)
(v)

3.15 Define the difference between market research and marketing research.

3.16 Setting a Strategic Marketing Plan involves four stages. These are

(i)
(ii)
(iii)
(iv)

3.17 What external analysis needs to be undertaken before developing a marketing strategy?

3.18 Explain, briefly, why marketing orientation is important to a modern organisation.

3.19 In the marketing mix, "Distribution" is usually classified as part of

A product
B price
C promotion
D place

3.20 The stages of the product lifecycle are

A initiation, contagion, maturity, decline
B introduction, review, maturity, decline
C introduction, growth, maturity, decline
D initiation, growth, maturity, decline

3.21 "Direct marketing" refers to

A a zero-level channel
B a one-level channel
C a two-level channel
D a multi-level channel

3.22 "M-marketing" (or "m-commerce") is

A marketing to men only
B marketing mature products
C marketing via mobile telephones
D marketing via multimedia

3.23 Canned foods and confectionery are normally classified as

A fast-moving consumer goods (FMCG)
B durables
C white goods
D brown goods

3.24 Age, gender and occupation are all examples of

A elements of the "promotion" part of the marketing mix
B markets
C segmentation variables
D marketing tools

3.25 Quality is primarily considered in which part of the marketing mix?

A Product
B Price
C Promotion
D Place

3.26 Television, newspapers and radio are all

A examples of e-commerce
B market segments
C advertising media
D examples of IT hardware

3.27 "Market shakeout" involves the weakest producers existing in a particular market and occurs in a period between

A growth through creativity and growth through direction
B introduction and market growth
C market growth and market maturity
D market maturity and decline

3.28 The choice to buy a fast-moving consumer good (FMCG) is normally

A a personal choice involving relatively low financial outlays
B a personal choice involving relatively high financial outlays
C a choice made on behalf of an organisation involving moderate outlays
D a personal choice influenced by new features, fashions and old product wearout

3.29 Analysing a market into sub-groups of potential customers with common needs and behaviours in order to target them through marketing techniques is called

A market research
B market development
C segmentation
D product adaptation

3.30 Separate people or groups such as initiators, influencers, buyers and users are all involved in a buying decision in the context of

A fast-moving consumer goods marketing
B business-to-business marketing
C business-to-consumer marketing
D services marketing

3.31 Charging a very low price on one item in order to generate customer loyalty and increased sales of other items is called

A market penetration
B loss leader pricing
C product penetration
D skim pricing

✓ Answers

3.1 C

3.2 (i) Product Orientation
(ii) Production Orientation
(iii) Sales Orientation
(iv) Marketing Orientation

3.3 (i) Product
(ii) Price
(iii) Promotion
(iv) Place

3.4 C

3.5 B2B means Business-to-business marketing and refers to the relationship between an organisation marketing/selling to another organisation. It is an important concept because it enables one to differentiate between consumer and business customers who co-operate and respond differently. B2B will have a much more complex Decision Making Unit (DMU), however, once you have them as a customer they tend to remain much more loyal than individual consumers. B2B customers are usually driven by factors other than price, such as quality or guaranteed delivery.

3.6 A

3.7 The traditional "push" marketing policy is concerned with promoting goods to wholesalers and retailers who then have the task of selling them to ultimate final customers. The emphasis of a push policy is, therefore, on getting dealers to accept goods and then "push" them to the final consumer.

A "pull" policy by comparison is one influencing final consumer attitudes so that a consumer demand is created which dealers are obliged to satisfy. A "pull" policy usually involves heavy expenditure on consumer advertising, but holds the potential of stimulating a much higher demand, by getting the customers to pull the product through the distribution chain.

3.8 (i) The economic view
(ii) The accounting view
(iii) The marketing view

3.9 D

3.10 B2C stands for Business-to-Consumer marketing and describes the most commonly perceived relationship. Here the marketing message is directed specifically to both the user and the Decision Making Unit (DMU). Since these are usually one and the same person, it is a much more direct relationship than B2B. B2C tends to be a much more volatile market than B2B and is much more price sensitive.

3.11 Market segmentation involves the subdividing of a market into distinct subgroups of customers, where any subgroup can be selected as a target market to be met with a distinct marketing mix.

3.12 C

3.13 Fast-moving consumer goods.

3.14 (i) Problems recognition
(ii) Information searching

(iii) Evaluation of alternatives
(iv) Purchasing decision
(v) Post-purchase evaluation

3.15 Market research is a concentration on one market alone.

Marketing research involves investigating all marketing activities – including an evaluation of the organisation's past and current performance.

3.16 (i) An investigation of the market and targeted segments.
(ii) Development of a PEST analysis.
(iii) Consideration of the organisation relative to PEST.
(iv) Developing an appropriate mix to achieve corporate aspirations

3.17 Externally you would need to analyse:

(i) Existing customers – What will their reaction be? Will it alienate any existing customers?
(ii) Potential customers – How many could there be?
(iii) The market – Can we segment the market? What is our position in the market? What is the position of other players?
(iv) Competitors – Who are they? How will they react? What are their strengths and weaknesses?

3.18 All organisations now operate in a diverse and rapidly changing environment. If an organisation is not aware of its customers, their needs, wants and desires and how these change over time, then their competitors will. This knowledge and understanding will enable the competitors to erode the competitive advantage originally enjoyed by the first company.

The concept of marketing orientation means that everyone is responsible for contributing to the marketing function and recognises the importance of delivering what the customer wants, in a manner that keeps them satisfied.

Without such awareness, organisations cannot hope to maintain their competitive advantage and consequent position within the market.

3.19 D

3.20 C

3.21 A

3.22 C

3.23 A

3.24 C

3.25 A

3.26 C

3.27 C

3.28 A

3.29 C

3.30 B

3.31 B

? Section B questions

Question 1

V is an innovative company run according to the principles of its entrepreneurial owner. V operates a package distribution service, a train service and sells holidays, bridal outfits, clothing, mobile telephones and soft drinks. V is well known for challenging the norm and "giving customers quality products and services at affordable prices and doing it all with a sense of fun". V spends little on advertising but has great brand awareness thanks to the "visibility" of its inspirational owner.

V has just announced the launch of "V-cosmetics" to exploit a gap in the market. The cosmetic range will be competitively priced against high street brands and have the distinctive V logo.

You work for a market analyst who is about to appear on a radio discussion of V's business interests. You have been asked to provide a clear, short briefing for the market analyst on the thinking behind V-cosmetics. Your research of the V-cosmetics range identifies innovative marketing proposals. V-cosmetics will not be on sale in shops, instead it will use two approaches to promotion and selling, namely:

- The use of "cosmetic associates". Individuals may apply to become an associate and, if accepted, will be required to buy a basic stock of every V-cosmetic product. The associate will then use these products as samples and "testers". After initial training associates organise parties in the homes of friends and their friends where they take orders for products at a listed price. Associates receive commission based on sales.
- The Internet and mobile telephone technology will also be heavily used to offer V-cosmetic products to the public.

Requirements

Prepare brief notes containing bullet points and no more than two to three sentences for each of the key points identified below. Use a separate page of your answer book for each key point (meaning that your notes are contained on no more than six pages in total).

(a) Explain how the proposed approach can be understood within the context of the marketing mix.

(5 marks)

(b) Explain the human resource implications of using "cosmetic associates".

(5 marks)

(c) Explain the concept of direct marketing.

(5 marks)

(d) Explain the advantages of the Internet as a marketing channel.

(5 marks)

(e) Describe how V might use the Internet and mobile phone technology as part of its marketing approach.

(5 marks)

(f) Identify the main ethical issues associated with the proposal to market V cosmetics.

(5 marks)

(Total = 30 marks)

Important note: Use a separate page of your answer book for each sub-question. You should limit your answer to each sub-question to no more than one page.

Section B questions

Answer 1

Requirement (a)

The marketing mix

The marketing mix involves four marketing tools; Product, Price, Promotion and Place that are "mixed/blended" in terms of effort, emphasis and integration. Here is V cosmetics' mix:

- Product. Good quality and branded products. They are likely to be attractive due to brand strength.
- Price. Competitive but not cheap (affordable). Price seems inflexible (list price). Are internet sales also placed at list price? Savings that V made on advertising, shops and expensive distribution networks can be passed on to customers. It can also reward associates and invest in IT. Likely to be profitable given saving potential over rivals.
- Promotion. Little advertising, focusing instead on Public Relations. Given success in other ventures, this should work with cosmetics. The strength of brand name is significant.
- Place that is getting the right products into the right places at the right time. Approach is through one level marketing (cosmetic associate) and interactive marketing. Assumes expertise of associates and user acceptance of the Internet. As philosophy is based on sense of fun, it may work. Need efficient distribution once an order is placed; link to V's distribution services?

Maybe a fifth P is relevant, that is People (see answer to Two (b)).

Key point: the mix must satisfy customer needs.

Requirement (b)

Human resource (HR) implications of cosmetic associates

The reputation of V is important and must be maintained through effective HR.

- Selection Criteria: Attitude applicants should (a) display a sense of fun and (b) reflect the image of the company. Trustworthiness is an important need for interview and references.
- Training of cosmetic associates in sales techniques and how to arrange parties. Also those servicing the Internet and text queries.
- Remuneration package needs to be right to attract and retain associates. Commission on sales must be sufficient incentive. Appropriate remuneration package for Internet sales needs to be devised.
- Supervision, monitoring and control: A system is needed (maybe customer question)

Requirement (c)

Direct Marketing

- A business, possibly manufacturer, deals directly with end customer, possibly using the Internet.
- A "zero level channel" that is direct between supplier and end customer.
- Shortens supply chain so takes costs out of value system.
- Examples include the web-based company Amazon.com and the direct booking of air travel online.
- Direct marketing mix implications for place and promotion. "Place" is not physical, it is cyberspace. Promotion is possible in electronic form through targeting web users.

Requirement (d)

Advantages of the Internet

- Speed of communication.
- Flexibility of use: promote, answer queries, sell, display products.
- Convenience for user: in own home and can be accessed any time.
- Attractive use of time for user: can compare and contrast prices and so on, with rivals "online".
- Potential for lower prices as costs are lower than physical stores with capital and running costs.
- Potential for companies to develop databases of customers; those making enquiries for further sales promotions.

Requirement (e)

Internet and mobile telephone

Internet

- Fits sense of fun – not a physical event (browsing, enquiries and purchasing online).
- Relies on user acceptance of credit cards; this is likely given other V businesses.
- Expectations that prices are cheaper than the high street; fits affordable prices philosophy.
- Orders online (needs efficient distribution once the order is placed, maybe linking to V's distribution services).
- Promotion using, for example, web banners, affiliation websites, collaboration with other websites and search facilities.

Mobile telephones ("M-marketing")

- To stimulate product interest, maybe through V mobiles links, text alerts and so on.
- As a sales alternative to the Internet. Novel: fits "sense of fun".
- Could be used to arrange a follow up by passing details on to associates.
- To deal with a range of customer enquiries. (Need sophisticated IT.)

Requirement (f)

Ethical issues

Ethical stance of an individual business is determined by organisational culture and philosophy.

- What we know about V: entrepreneurial (takes risks?), different, quality products, affordable prices and fun. These factors will be relevant as will legislative frameworks.
- Issue of using associates: are they being fairly treated? (Requirement to buy basic stock, continue to sell products, is remuneration appropriate?)
- Issues of using parties for selling: (Other examples: Tupperware, Virgin Vie, Ann Summers.) Is the public being tricked/pressured into using their home in this way? What is in it for them (gifts, discounts, fees and so on.).
- Issue of selling approach: are associates obliged to adopt impolite or "pushy" sales techniques, which is unfair on the customer.
- Issue of targeting customers through Internet and mobiles: may be overly intrusive or abuse of databases/relationship (with possible implications for data protection legislation).

Section C questions

Question 1

For an in-house marketing research training day with your team, you have been asked to produce a handout that

(a) Explains the difference between qualitative and quantitative methods of marketing research.

(4 marks)

(b) Provides a list of clear examples of the different tools used to gather different types of marketing research.

(6 marks)

(c) Gives advantages and disadvantages of each example listed in (b).

(12 marks)

(d) Provides a clear illustrative example of how and why you would prefer a qualitative approach as opposed to a quantitative approach in conducting marketing research.

(8 marks)
(Total = 30 marks)

Question 2

CM's founder first began producing breakfast food from a start-up unit on a small industrial estate. Now CM is the market leader in Europe and Oceania. Once established in Europe, the company made the breakthrough into Oceania thanks to demand from ex-pats and contacts with a family member who happened to be a director of a supermarket chain in Australia. The company's founder is very "hands on" and has made all the major strategic decisions to date based on intuition.

CM spends heavily on promoting most of its 20 products on television, normally before and after childrens' programmes with high viewing figures. Research conducted 10 years ago shows that children love small gifts contained within packs and the association of certain of the products to cartoon characters. CM also manufactures its most popular lines and packages them as "own brand" alternatives for some large supermarket chains. These sell more cheaply than CM-branded products, are less costly to produce (they contain inexpensive packaging and no gifts) but sales remain low.

CM is now facing a more uncertain environment with increasing competition (from a North American firm), sales levels that seem to have peaked and the prospect of the founder retiring very soon. Management consultants advising CM have identified a need to develop a structured marketing strategic plan for the organisation and for greater involvement of other staff in future strategic decisions. As a further complication, CM has recently received some adverse publicity from an international health "watchdog" body that claims that CM's products contain potentially harmful levels of both sugar and salt.

Requirements

(a) Evaluate CM's situation making specific mention of marketing and ethical issues.

(15 marks)

(b) Explain how CM might develop a marketing strategic plan.

(15 marks)

(Total = 30 marks)

✓ Section C questions

Answer 1

This training session will focus on the two methods of marketing research. These are qualitative and quantitative.

(a) *Qualitative*: Qualitative methods are an approach to try to understand the attitudes and motivations behind an individual's purchase decision. In order to do this, we have to see into their thought processes and understand their psychology. Qualitative methods allow the subject to offer their feelings, attitudes and preferences, rather than just an opinion without knowing why. Qualitative methods require interaction between the interviewee and the subject and are, therefore, very personal. Because of this the interviewer has to be extremely well trained and has to understand their role. They should not prompt or sway the subject but encourage them to feel relaxed and in control.

Quantitative: Quantitative methods of marketing research consist of a straight relationship between the subject and their opinion. We are not interested in the motivation/reasons behind the opinion. Due to this, the method is less personal and more straightforward. The questions are pre-determined and there is no room for expansion. The responses are normally either one-word answers or merely a tick in a box to indicate preference. The interviewer merely selects a candidate.

To help clarify the difference between qualitative and quantitative, I have listed the different tools that can be used to collect such data.

(b) *Qualitative*

Questionnaires – semi-structured
– unstructured
Possibly telephone or face to face to allow and enable interaction
Projective techniques – word association
Focus groups (6 to 10)
Depth interviews (1 to 1)

Quantitative

Questionnaires – structured
– semi-structured
Probably electronic or postal
Electronic meters – such as customer counter on shop doors
Observation
Electronic point of sale

(c) There are, however, advantages and disadvantages to each of the techniques that have been mentioned.

Qualitative methods

Questionnaires

Advantages: Can gain a lot of information about the reason why a purchase is made/not made. Insight into people's motivations.

Disadvantages: May obtain a lot of irrelevant information. Answers can sometimes be difficult to code and therefore mistakes may happen.

Projective techniques

Advantages: These are highly psychological and can be more indicative of hidden feelings. Instead of being able to say what people think the interviewer might want to hear, they are asked to describe a picture, or react to a word. The subject does not really have time to think, therefore true meanings are revealed.

Disadvantages: Due to the nature of the information, a highly trained individual has to interpret the responses.

Focus groups

Advantages: Discussion is formal and a variety of opinions can be heard. With prompting from the interviewer, subjects can interact with each other, revealing deeper meanings.

Disadvantages: The interviewer needs to create a relaxed environment where people feel comfortable. If this is not done, conversation may be limited and may be a waste of time.

Depth interviews

Advantages: These are completed on a one-to-one basis and a lengthy discussion can be formulated gaining detailed knowledge.

Disadvantages: The interviewer needs to prompt but not control the situation and needs to make sure useless information is not collected.

Quantitative methods

Questionnaires

Advantages: They are easy to interpret, as all answers are pre-coded.

Disadvantages: Do not hear the subject's motivations; have to make sure questions are correct to begin with. Non-response from postal surveys. Inaccurate decoding and analysis of results.

Electronic meters

Advantages: No room for error. Normally used for counting people going into shops or past a particular point.

Disadvantages: Of limited use.

Observation

Advantages: Interviewer has easy task of merely recording customers' presence.

Disadvantages: Limited use, does not reveal motivations.

EPOS

Advantages: Can be used to gather data about customers' buying habits. How often they purchase, what they purchase and with electronic point of sale, how they like to purchase. It can help decide relationships with buying patterns and be useful for sales/marketing team.

Disadvantages: Too much information may be gathered. A system needs to be installed in order to extract useful information and what to do with it.

(d) In summary I would like to confirm that my preferred method of collecting marketing research is the qualitative approach. This is because it is the events leading up to the purchase that marketers are interested in and which are the most complicated. Quantitative methods do not provide insight into the motivation of consumers, which is extremely important in formulating the marketing mix. As long as the interviewer is trained in their role and answers our analyses correctly, qualitative marketing research is extremely beneficial to the company. Quantitative techniques are extremely limited and only provide marketers with the obvious. Qualitative techniques provide insight to the buying process such as AWARENESS, EVALUATION, TRIAL, ADOPTION. It is these which encourage consumers to buy products and the quicker a customer is moved through these stages the quicker a product is purchased.

Answer 2

Requirements (a)

Situation evaluation.

Major challenges

CM is said to be facing three major challenges:

- Increasing competition
- Sales levels that seem to have "peaked"
- The prospect of the retirement of the key decision maker

Competition

CM is the market leader in breakfast food manufacture in Europe and Oceania but is facing increasing competition (from N. America). CM appears to have no presence on the other continents, making it an international rather than global player. Although diets vary across continents it is likely that the North American diet is (at least) similar. This means that potentially other firms are supplying the American market and these competitors could be powerful and have the ability to challenge CM's leadership in its own markets, CM needs to decide how it responds to this threat from international competition. There is no information on the basis upon which CM's competitors marketing mix varies from its own. If an alternative mix to CM is apparently proving more successful, then CM should re-examine its own mix accordingly. (See later)

More positively CM should recognise that potential markets on other continents exist and these represent opportunities for development.

Sales

Sales levels seem to have "peaked". One interpretation can be drawn from an understanding of the concept of the market life cycle. When the life cycle of a market reaches so-called "maturity" stage, demand will have reached its limit. If this is the case, CM should consider new products or new markets before the market life moves into the "decline" stage. In terms of product range CM has a portfolio of twenty product items, but it is unclear how often this range is "refreshed". Reference to potential new markets, maybe outside Europe and Oceania, has been made to earlier.

Decision making (and Strategic Marketing approach)

CM's founder, as the key decision maker, is retiring soon. He/she is credited with growing CM to its present size from a business "start-up" operation. He/she is very "hands on" and has made all the major strategic decisions to date based on intuition. (It is apparent that there is no structured strategic marketing plan.) The development into another geographical market typically seems to have resulted through good fortune and market demand rather than rational decision making and promotional efforts. (CM made the breakthrough into Oceania thanks to demand from experts and contacts with a family member who happened to be a director of a supermarket chain in Australia.) Organisationally, it is difficult to continue operating in this way, particularly with the retirement of the founder. Although the organisational culture could properly be described as entrepreneurial, CM's sheer size may mean that some of the spirit is in any case diminishing.

This can in part be explained by reference to Greiner's organisational growth model (1972). Under this model, firms can experience evolutionary growth which eventually leads to a situation of revolutionary crisis, when the organisation's ways of doing things become less effective. The implication of this thinking is that change is unavoidable and ways of overcoming each crisis need to be determined for the organisation to continue growing. Under the model, the first phase of growth is achieved by some creative idea, product or service that enables the organisation to become established in the market place. A crisis occurs when the entrepreneur's informal and personal approach to managing the business simply cannot cope with its increased size. This crisis of leadership appears to have been reached within CM. If the organisation can adopt more formal systems of management, (in CM's case strategic marketing); there will be a basis for further growth through "direction".

Other issues

Ethical issues

The adverse publicity from an international health "watchdog" body that claims that CM's products contain potentially harmful levels of both sugar and salt raises ethical concerns. CM spends "heavily" on TV advertising and undoubtedly the target audience for CM's promotional effort is children as it advertises before and after childrens' programmes. The inclusion of small gifts contained within packs and the association of certain of the products to cartoon characters and expensive packaging confirms as much. Children influence their parents to purchase the product. The ethical issues are as follows:

- Is it "right" that promotion is based upon children placing demands on their parents, particularly if their parents cannot afford to buy the product?
- The sugar and salt content are apparently important in achieving a taste that children like. Is it ethical to manufacture and sell products that might be unhealthy to vulnerable children.

- The adverse publicity may impact upon sales, CM will need to decide how it responds to these claims, for instance:
  - Conduct its own research and possibly challenge the watchdog claims.
  - Discredit the findings and the body making the claims.
  - Modify its product content so there is less salt and sugar present.
  - Increase promotion to compensate any fall off in sales as a result of adverse publicity.

Product nature

There is good reason for believing that the associated features and packaging is the most significant product feature, specifically:

- Past research confirms that children love small gifts contained within packs and the association of certain of the products to cartoon characters.
- Some products are sold as "own brand" alternatives for some large supermarket chains.

Although these sell more cheaply than CM-branded products, they are less costly to produce as they contain inexpensive packaging and no free gifts. The minimal sales underline the point that packaging and advertising are crucial.

Marketing mix

CM's current marketing mix has evidently developed over time and seems to be the product of decisions made by the company's founder. CM can properly be described as a "marketing-oriented" organisation as it has a main focus of the customer (children) and their demands. The mix exhibits in particular product features and packaging, promotion through expensive advertising, and (using the fifth P of the marketing mix) the founder as the key person. In terms of place, sales are through supermarkets and based on two continents. The price reflects high promotional costs and expensive packaging.

Requirements (b)

Developing a marketing strategic plan for CM,

An important point, particularly given CM's own position of a lack of formal strategy and the past influence of a single person (the founder), is that a range of people from within the organisation should be involved. Although marketing specialists might lead processes, all functional areas should participate in developing the strategy. This is important so that there is ownership, realism and co-ordination.

In order for CM to develop a Marketing Strategic Plan, a number of key processes will need to be undertaken concurrently and are identified below.

Identify and articulate CM's corporate objectives and the role that marketing can play in achieving them

Conduct an audit of the external environment

This will involve a detailed investigation of the following:

- The market for manufactured breakfast food.
- The market segments which CM is interested in (e.g. European childrens' eating habits and preferences).
- The trends influencing the market, typically using a PEST (political economic, sociocultural and technological) framework for analysis*. A consideration of CM's position relative to the most significant factors (including potential realistic ways in which the organisation might influence such factors) should be undertaken

- The activities, strategic capability and strengths and weaknesses of competitors.
- Future potential scenarios and trends, possibly using industry and other experts.

Conduct an internal analysis

This will clarify what CM wants to achieve over the planning period and its capability, specifically:

- The identification of the factors that contribute towards CM's strengths and weaknesses.

These internal factors are controllable and may lead to the development of targets,

- The agreement of corporate aspirations including specific marketing objectives and SMART (specific, measurable, achievable, realistic and time bound) targets.

Synthesis and discussion

Some of the main factors arising from the above processes might be synthesised into a SWOT (strengths, weaknesses, opportunities and threats) analysis. (SW are internal and OT external factors.)

Discussions should focus on developing an appropriate mix of marketing factors to achieve CM's objectives in the light of earlier analysis; this will include any actions necessary to bridge gaps between expectations and capability. Specifically, the mix will address future actions relating to pricing issues, promotional activity, place and product features.

Communication and co-ordination

A strategy can ultimately be developed. It will however need to be carefully co-ordinated with other functional strategies including Finance, IT and HR.

The strategy should be written, approved by CM's decision makers and clearly communicated to the workforce. The strategy will include:

- Clear marketing goals and objectives.
- Targets, measures and performance indicators,
- The costing of the plan and the development of a revenue budget.
- An identification and costing of any capital requirements.
- Identification of strategic alternatives,
- A detailed action plan.

* Other alternative frameworks might be used including PESTEL which also recognises environmental and legal factors and so on.

4

Managing Human Capital

Managing Human Capital

4

LEARNING OUTCOMES

This chapter concerns an organisation's most unpredictable yet powerful resource: its human resource. The successful management of this, the most valuable of all assets, occupies the segment of the syllabus carrying the heaviest weighting (of 30%). By completing this chapter and the associated readings and questions, it should help you to:

- explain the role of the human resource management (HRM) function and its relationship to other parts of the organisation;
- produce and explain a HR plan and supporting practices;
- evaluate organisational recruitment, selection, induction, appraisal, training and career planning activities;
- identify features of a HR plan that vary depending on organisation type and employment model.
- evaluate the role of incentives in staff development as well as individual and organisational performance;
- explain the importance of ethical behaviour in business in general and for the Chartered Management Accountant, in particular.

? Questions

4.1 Define motivation.

4.2 Schein identified four categories of worker. These were

(i)
(ii)
(iii)
(iv)

4.3 McGregor's Theory X and Theory Y stated:

(i) *X Theory*:
(ii) *Y Theory*:

4.4 Briefly describe Maslow's hierarchy of needs.

4.5 What are the limitations of Maslow's hierarchy of needs?

4.6 Which of the following would not contribute towards motivating a team:

A Job design
B Management style
C Groups and teamwork
D Punishing poor performance

4.7 When considering whether to change to PRP, an employer should consider all of the following except:

A Does it measure performance adequately?
B Does it encourage productivity?
C Does a competing company already offer its employees PRP?
D Is it controllable?

4.8 Define Human Resource Management (HRM).

4.9 Guest identified the six components linking HRM and strategy. These are

(i)
(ii)
(iii)
(iv)
(v)
(vi)

4.10 Describe five elements that make up Devanna et al.'s model of the HRM cycle.

4.11 Human resource planning should be undertaken for all of the following reasons except:

A It gives the HR manager something to do
B It helps to rationally plan recruitment
C It enables budgets to be established
D It enables succession planning

4.12 What will have the most significant impact upon an HR strategy?

A An increase in the cost of labour
B A change in labour legislation
C An increase in the productivity of the existing workforce
D A change in the corporate objectives of the organisation

4.13 Identify the activities in the HR cycle.

4.14 Define what an assessment centre is and explain why an organisation should consider utilising one?

4.15 Why is the appraisal process important?

4.16 What are the components of a good systematic training system?

4.17 Name four different types of appraisal.

4.18 The following are all problems associated with succession planning except:

A Retention
B Timing
C Pay
D Performance appraisal

4.19 Why has there been great interest in flexible employment patterns over recent years?

4.20 "Scientific Management" was developed by

A Taylor
B Herzberg
C Maslow
D McGregor

4.21 Douglas McGregor concluded that there are two sets of assumptions about the attitudes of staff. These are

A theory A and theory B
B theory X and theory Y
C theory Y and theory Z
D theory E and theory O

4.22 Which of the following statements is true, according to Herzberg?

A Money is a motivator
B Food is a motivator
C Work is a motivator
D Status is a motivator

4.23 Which of the following dislike work?

A Theory X staff
B Theory Y staff
C Self-actualising man
D Rational-economic man

4.24 Expectancy theory is an example of

A a content theory of motivation
B a process theory of motivation
C a system theory of motivation
D a rational-economic theory of motivation

4.25 In human resource planning, retirement and resignation are examples of

A staff increases
B natural wastage
C staff costs
D planned exit

4.26 During the selection process, the skills, experience and characteristics of job applicants should be compared to the

A job description
B personal statement
C job analysis
D person specification

4.27 The "seven-point plan" is a tool used for

A manpower planning
B conducting appraisals
C creating a person specification
D determining salary levels

4.28 When someone commences a new job, the process of familiarisation is known as

A probationary period.
B recruitment.
C appraisal.
D induction.

4.29 An effective appraisal system involves

A assessing the personality of the appraisee.
B a process initiated by the manager who needs an update from the appraisee.
C advising on the faults of the appraisee.
D a participative, problem-solving process between the manager and appraisee.

4.30 Vroom's motivation theory is calculated to assess

A the knowledge of an individual.
B the satisfaction with work.
C the choice of alternatives to satisfy needs
D the quality of work performed.

4.31 Job rotation involves

A a redesign of a person's post based upon job analysis.
B the movement of an individual to another post in order to gain experience.
C the expansion and enrichment of a person's job content.
D the relocation of a post holder in order to benefit from the experience of a number of potential mentors.

4.32 A grievance procedure is established by an organisation in order that

A there is a standing process to deal with the arbitration of disputes
B the organisation can fairly discipline members of the workforce for wrongdoing
C the workforce might formally raise issues where ill treatment has occurred
D collective bargaining between the employer's side and the workforce might proceed smoothly

4.33 An "assessment centre" approach is used

A as part of an appraisal process
B as part of a process of training and development
C as part of a selection process
D as part of an exit interview process

4.34 Selection tests that fail to produce similar results over time when taken by the same candidate are

A contradictory
B unreliable
C too general
D unstable

4.35 Training workers in methods of statistical process control and work analysis

A overcomes a crisis of control in an organisation's life cycle
B is part of a succession planning approach to Human Resources
C is part of a quality management approach
D is part of a scientific management approach

4.36 The use of standard questions in job interviews helps ensure

A fairness
B validity
C reliability
D completeness

4.37 The so-called "psychological contract" is a notion that is based on

A segmenting then accessing a market
B the buyer/supplier relationship
C a distinctive style of testing used in selection procedures
D the expectations the organisation and employee have of one another

4.38 The processes of job analysis and individual performance appraisal are related in the sense that

A they are different terms for the same process
B performance appraisal is based on job analysis
C both form part of the selection process
D job analysis is based on performance appraisal

4.39 Content theories of motivation tend to focus mainly on

A the needs of the group
B feelings of complacency or dissatisfaction
C the needs of individuals
D the use of "carrots" and "sticks" as devices

4.40 It is the role of "outplacement consultants" to

A provide help to redundant employees including training and finding jobs
B provide help to employees wishing to gain experience in other roles
C arrange for placing products in an untested market place
D arrange for placing under-used assets at the disposal of start up businesses

4.41 F. W. Taylor's thinking on motivation in the workplace involved a belief that

A social groups and individuals as part of a culture should be key considerations
B reward for effort and workplace efficiency should be key considerations
C managers had two different sets of assumptions about their subordinates
D "motivators" and "hygiene factors" should be key considerations

4.42 In terms of employment CIMA's ethical guidelines require members to

A act responsibly in the way that all other professionals do
B act responsibly but in a way that satisfies organisational demands and pressures
C act responsibly but in a way that satisfies the individual's own ethical code
D act responsibly, honour any legal contract of employment and conform to employment legislation

4.43 360 degree feedback is part of a system that encourages

A organisational appraisal based on feedback from customers and suppliers
B organisational appraisal based on relative industry and competitor performance
C personal appraisal based on feedback from peers, subordinates, line managers and even external parties
D personal appraisal based on line manager feedback and self-appraisal documentation

4.44 "Spot rates" normally refer to a specific pay rate determined by reference to

A the market place
B incremental progression
C a negotiated point on a pay spine
D experience and qualifications of a newly recruited person

4.45 In the expectancy theory of motivation "valence" refers to

A a belief that an outcome will satisfy organisational tasks
B a person's own preference for achieving a particular outcome
C a belief that the outcome will be shared by others equally
D an understanding of the probability of an event happening.

✓ Answers

4.1 Motivation is the internal psychological process of initiating, energising, directing and maintaining goal-directed behaviours.

4.2 (i) Rational/Economic Man
(ii) Social Man
(iii) Self-actualising Man
(iv) Complex Man

4.3 *Theory X*: Work is inherently distasteful to most people. The average human being prefers to be directed, wishes to avoid responsibility and wants security above all else.

Theory Y: People want to contribute to meaningful goals they have helped to establish. The average human being learns under the right conditions not only to accept but to seek responsibility.

4.4 Abraham Maslow constructed his theory of motivation as a result of his experience as a clinical psychologist. The theory is found on three fundamental assumptions:

1 The individual is "a perpetually wanting animal";
2 Only relatively unsatisfied needs are capable of motivating behaviour;
3 Five levels of needs, he identified, are arranged in a hierarchy of potency. This means that at any one time, the lowest level of relatively unsatisfied need will be the one that motivates current behaviour, and the less it is satisfied the more it will motivate. The individual will act primarily in order to satisfy that need, and then move on to the next level and so on.

The hierarchy of needs is as follows:

Higher-order needs

5. Self-actualisation
4. Esteem
3. Affiliation (social)
2. Safety and security
1. Physiological

Lower-order needs

As each need is satisfied, the individual moves up the hierarchy, with successive levels of need dominating behaviour. If conditions are favourable, the individual will progress towards self-actualisation, unless a lower-order need again becomes unsatisfied, in which case behaviour will revert to seeking satisfaction of this need.

4.5 Maslow's hierarchy of needs does have some limitations. The main ones are

- It is very difficult to test empirically.
- It assumes that all individuals have the same needs organised in the same way.
- It is difficult to predict actual behaviour from the theory.

4.6 D

4.7 C

4.8 Bratton and Gold (1999) defined HRM as:

That part of the management process that specialises in the management of people in work organisations. HRM emphasises that employees are critical to achieving sustainable competitive advantage, that human resources practices need to be integrated with the corporate strategy, and that human resource specialists help organisational controllers to meet both efficiency and equity objectives.

4.9
(i) an HRM strategy
(ii) a set of HRM practices
(iii) a set of HRM outcomes
(iv) behavioural outcomes
(v) a number of performance outcomes
(vi) financial outcomes

4.10

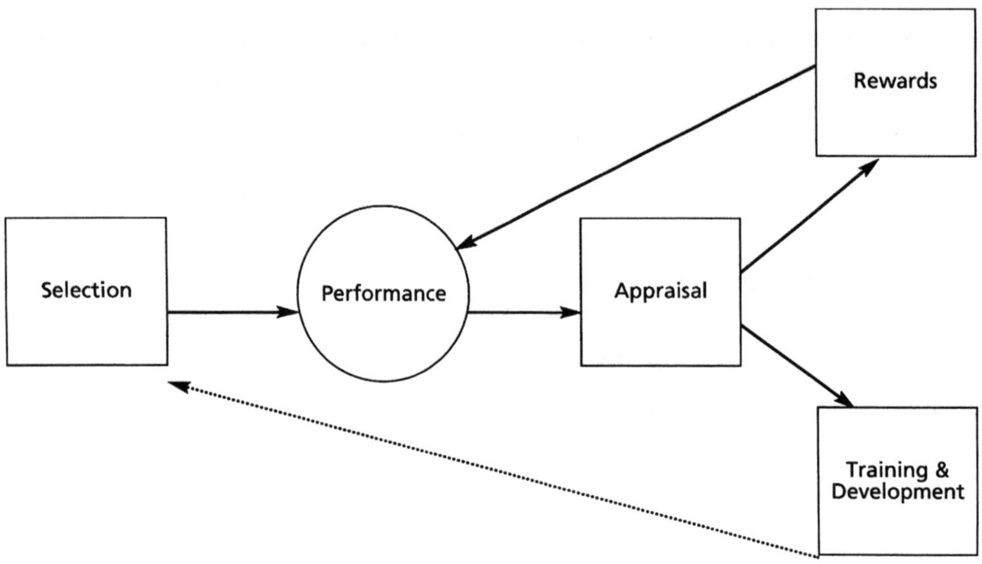

The human resource cycle

The four HR activities of selection, appraisal, training and rewards aim to increase the fifth element, organisational performance. The model emphasised the coherence of internal HRM policies and the importance of matching internal HRM policies and practices to the organisation's external business strategy. The cycle represents a simple model that serves as a useful framework for explaining the nature and significance of key HR practices and the interactions among the factors making up the complex field of HRM.

It is important to note that the overall performance of the organisation depends on efficient and effective operation of each of the four components and the co-ordination of each with the organisation's strategy:

1 The selection process is important to ensure that the organisation obtains people with the right skills and/or the potential to develop such skills.
2 Appraisal is a pivotal process enabling managers to set targets for future performance, in line with an organisation's strategic objectives. It also enables managers to

assess the gap between the competences already possessed by staff and the skills and knowledge that the staff will require in order for the organisation to attain its strategic objectives.

3 Training and development are essential to ensure that staff can compete with the best in the industry in terms of their ability to develop key competences. It is in this sense that their skills are a key source of competitive advantage.

4 The reward system has to be such as to motivate people and to ensure that those key employees do not leave the organisation and join the competition.

4.11 A

4.12 D

4.13 This consist of:

- job analysis
- job description
- person specifications
- recruitment
- selection
- induction
- review and evaluation.
- termination.

4.14 An assessment centre involves "the assessment of a group of individuals by a team of judges using a comprehensive and interrelated series of techniques".

An assessment centre does not necessarily mean a physical centre but is a particular approach and philosophy.

A typical assessment centre will involve applicants attending for 1 or 2 days and being subjected to a "battery" of selection techniques. Trained assessors will observe candidates and at the end of the exercise will pool their judgements of the applicants based on their performance on the range of selection devices and an overall assessment of each individual's suitability will then be reached.

Although assessment centres can be very accurate methods of selection, they are obviously expensive and can only be justified for certain types of jobs. However, the reason that organisations should consider utilising them is because research shows that "the probability of selecting an 'above average performer' on a random basis was 15%, a figure that rose to 35% using appraisal and interview data and to *76% using assessment centre results.*"

4.15 The appraisal process is important because it is a means by which both employer and employee can validate strengths and weaknesses and agree approaches to train and develop the individual to become more efficient and effective.

Appraisals are often perceived negatively by many members of staff – possibly as the result of a poor personal experience. The process should be open, fair and productive. The outcome should be an agreed programme to assist an individual improve their effectiveness and efficiency, thereby enabling the organisation to become more effective and efficient – a win/win situation.

4.16 It should include methods of ensuring the following:

- the determination of training needs;
- identification of training objectives;
- development of criteria against which to assess performance;
- development of methods to determine current levels of proficiency among potential trainees to enable the right people to be selected for training;
- arrangements for the location, type and duration of the training;
- methods for actually carrying out the training and encouraging effective learning;
- consideration of ways of monitoring the effectiveness of the training and comparing outcomes against criteria.

4.17
- Self-appraisal;
- Supervisor/appraisee;
- 180 degree;
- 360 degree.

4.18 C

4.19 The following reasons may explain why there is a great interest in flexible employment practices:

- lower labour costs through operating at lower manning levels;
- growing international competitiveness is said to have made flexibility a necessity;
- improved responsiveness to market changes;
- greater utilisation of equipment;
- higher quality output;
- possibility of lower batch sizes tailored to specific market segments;
- organisational flexibility to adapt, innovate, diversify and divest;
- greater control of labour processes and costs.

4.20 A

4.21 B

4.22 C

4.23 A

4.24 B

4.25 B

4.26 D

4.27 C

4.28 D

4.29 D

4.30 C

4.31 B

4.32 C

4.33 C

4.34 B

4.35 C

4.36 A

4.37 D

4.38 B

4.39 C

4.40 A

4.41 B

4.42 D

4.43 C

4.44 A

4.45 B

? Section B questions

Question 1

X is a large retailer, specialising in the sale of home furnishings (such as beds, chairs and tables). X has twenty-five retail outlets, each of which is sited in a major city in X's home country. X employs almost three hundred staff, as follows:

- Eight directors, each of whom is responsible for a different function of the business.
- Four regional sales managers, each of whom is responsible for between six and eleven retail outlets.
- Twenty-eight store managers, three of whom provide cover for holidays and sickness.
- Fifty assistant store managers, two in each store.
- Over seventy supervisors, who are each responsible for a department of a store.
- About one hundred full- and part-time sales staff.
- Thirty head office administration staff.

The regional sales manager for the Western region has recently resigned, and is due to leave X in three weeks. The HR manager needs to recruit a replacement, as none of the store managers are believed to have the required skills and experience to do the job. As this is the first time X has recruited a regional sales manager from outside the organisation, the HR manager needs some help.

Requirements

(a) Identify five benefits, to X, of human resource planning.

(5 marks)

(b) Describe the techniques of "staff development", "promotion" and "succession planning", explaining their relevance to the operations of X.

(5 marks)

(c) Explain what is meant by "job analysis", and how X should carry out such a process.

(5 marks)

(d) Explain what is meant by a "person specification", and its role in the recruitment process.

(5 marks)

(e) Identify the likely content of a person specification, using Rodgers' 7-point plan, for the regional sales manager vacancy.

(5 marks)

(f) Identify the steps in a recruitment and selection process to be used when recruiting a new regional sales manager.

(5 marks)
(Total = 30 marks)

✓ Section B questions

Answer 1

(a) The benefits of human resource planning, to X, are as follows:

1 To establish budgets in order to control costs.
2 To plan for recruitment, so it can be managed more effectively.
3 To improve the management of redeployment, redundancy and retirement.
4 To plan the education, development and training of the workforce.
5 To plan succession.
6 To adapt to changing circumstances.

(Note: only five are required)

(b) Staff development is the process of planning and implementing a system whereby existing staff can progress in their careers. It utilises the appraisal system to ensure that staff receive any training that they need, thus gaining new skills and remaining motivated. In X, plans can be put in place for each sales assistant, to ensure that they gradually gain the skills and experience needed to become supervisor, assistant manager and store manager.

Promotion, in HR terms, is the process of appointing a member of staff to a job higher up the hierarchy. In X this would include appointing one of the store managers to the vacancy for a regional sales manager.

Succession planning is the process of planning to ensure that it is unnecessary to recruit any staff from outside the organisation. It uses information from the staff development process to plan which members of staff will be promoted to which jobs at what point in time. X could have used succession planning to avoid having to recruit a regional sales manager from outside the organisation.

(c) Job analysis is the process of analysing a vacancy to determine whether it should be filled and to define the nature of the job and the type of person required to fill it. Job analysis leads logically to the preparation of a job description and person specification. A job can be analysed by a number of methods, including the following:

1 Direct observation of the person doing the job.
2 Interviewing the existing post holder (the other regional sales managers).
3 Interviewing the immediate superior (the directors).
4 A manager trying the job.
5 Reading previous job descriptions.
6 Questionnaires (to the other regional sales managers).

(d) A person specification is a description of the "ideal candidate" for any job vacancy. It is created at the same time as a job description, but describes the person, rather than the tasks they are to perform. The person specification lists the skills and attributes of the ideal candidate, and can be used as a checklist when writing an advertisement or interviewing potential candidates.

(e) Using the Rodgers 7-point plan, a person specification for the regional sales manager position might include the following:

- Physical make-up: Good health, smart appearance, clear communicator.
- Attainments: educated to advanced level, possibly with a degree in sales and/or marketing.
- General intelligence: Above average.
- Special aptitudes: Car driver, experience of supervising large sales forces, experience in furnishings.
- Interests: customer service, human behaviour, anything target-oriented.
- Disposition: Calm, not liable to stress, willing to commit to the goals of the business.
- Circumstances: Living in the region, willing to travel a lot and stay away from home.

(f) The steps in the recruitment and selection process are as follows:

- Advertisement of the job vacancy: The vacancy should be advertised in a local or national newspaper, or a furniture trade journal.
- Preliminary contact: Applicants should be asked to submit a CV/résumé or application form.
- Initial screening: Applications should be compared to the person specification, in order to reject any obviously unsuitable applicants.
- Interviewing: Shortlisted candidates should be interviewed, probably by a director, another regional sales manager and someone from the HR department.
- Testing: X might use aptitude and personality tests, to support the selection process.
- Selection: The job should be offered to the most suitable candidate.

Section C questions

Question 1

The T City Police Force has been subjected to considerable criticism in recent years. The first criticism is from *some* of the citizens of T City who claim racial harassment and slow response to emergency calls. The second is from a government audit which found that the T City Police Force had a poorer record on crime prevention and convictions for crime than any of the other nine urban forces in the country.

As well as a number of other measures, the T City Chief of Police has accepted a recommendation from the head of HR to implement a performance appraisal system linked to a performance-related payment (PRP) system. A spokesman for the Association of Police Officers has objected to the proposed appraisal and PRP systems on the grounds that limited government funding and the poor socio-economic conditions of T City district will make the system unworkable.

Requirements

(a) Explain the purpose of performance appraisal. Discuss how the T City Police Force could use the information from the performance appraisal system to improve the performance of its police officers.

(12 marks)

(b) In the light of the comments made by the spokesman for the Association of Police Officers, discuss the potential problems associated with the introduction of the proposed performance appraisal system and PRP system.

(18 marks)
(Total = 30 marks)

Question 2

The F Company is engaged in the insurance business, an area where technological change has driven reorganisation. Developments in information technology have produced a situation where clerical level employees, rather than professionals, can now adequately perform activities which once required many years of training and work experience.

One effect has been the replacement of many skills required by insurance professionals and sales personnel, which had traditionally formed two of the main career streams in F Company. On the sales side, the employment of a highly skilled sales force has been at least partly replaced by the greater use of self-employed commission-only sales personnel but the use of telephone call centres has also had a major impact in reducing the number of sales personnel required. The type of work in the call centres is by its very nature repetitive, routine and boring.

Among the insurance professionals, the increasing sophistication of the software in use has increasingly meant their replacement by part-time clerical employees, with general keyboard skills and much less extensive training specific to the company.

Requirements

(a) Explain the implications of the technological changes in F Company for succession and career planning.

(14 marks)

(b) Using any appropriate theory of motivation, assess the impact of the changes in F Company on the motivation of both trainee insurance professionals and company sales personnel. Recommend ways for motivating staff employed in the new telephone call centres.

(16 marks)
(Total = 30 marks)

Question 3

The discovery of heavily overstated profits in some of the largest US corporations in 2002 undermined investor confidence in company accounts and called into question the integrity of senior managers, their professional staff and the presumed independence of external auditors.

Requirements

(a) Describe the *key influences on* the ethical conduct of senior management of business corporations, their professional staff and those involved with auditing their accounts.

(12 marks)

(b) Explain what both businesses and professional bodies can do to influence the ethical behaviour of their organisational members.

(18 marks)
(Total = 30 marks)

Question 4

B plc, a large manufacturing company, is currently facing major problems in how to motivate its workforce.

For years, the company used share incentives to motivate its otherwise low-paid employees. This method worked very well during the period of the company's growth in the 1990s as the value of the shares offered to employees at a 20% discount increased in value year on year. Employees felt that their contribution was paying off for the company and for themselves and, as a result, tended to be highly motivated and loyal.

The start of the new century, however, has not been kind to the company. Increased competition has resulted in a decline in revenues and profits, and the share price of the company has been on a downward trend. This decline has significantly reduced the value of the individual portfolios which employees have amassed through the generous share incentive scheme. The company has noticed recently that the motivation and loyalty of employees have begun to decline.

The problems that B plc has experienced in its use of the share incentive scheme are quite common, but companies continue to make use of them.

Requirements

(a) Describe a theory of motivation on which such incentive schemes are based, and explain the merits and limitations of the theory you have described.

(18 marks)

(b) Explain the advantages and limitations of the share incentive schemes, and suggest ways in which financial rewards could be tied more closely to employee performance.

(12 marks)

(Total = 30 marks)

Section C questions

Answer 1

(a) The purpose of any performance appraisal system is primarily to improve the performance of individuals to whom it is applied, but this can be broken down in a number of subsidiary objectives. Appraisal can be used to identify current performance, provide feedback, increase motivation, identify training and development needs, assess the case for salary increases and indicate to employees what they need to do to improve their performance.

The information gathered from a formal and informal appraisal system about the performance of individual police officers can contribute to more efficient and effective processes of selection, development and reward systems in a way that will improve the collective performance of the whole T City Police Force.

In the case of *selection*, information from formal appraisal interviews and from informal appraisals by his or her superiors about the officer's performance can assist in the selection of officers for promotion to higher ranks in the Force. To the extent that officers are promoted with the special competences to deal with the particular problems facing the force, then the performance of the T City Police Force should improve.

With regard to *training and development*, the appraisal process is most useful in providing information on the training and development needs of officers. Such needs can be determined by estimating the gap between the individual officer's current skills and competences and the demands placed on officers by the new strategies and policies developed by senior officers to deal with residents' complaints and the deficiencies identified by the government audit.

The information derived from appraisals can also assist in the determination of what *performance-related payments* (PRP) should be made to officers who meet their agreed objectives. This system of linking appraisal with financial rewards can be used to motivate police officers to greater efforts in meeting the targets set for them by superiors.

Given the way in which selection, training and development and rewards can be improved by information from the selection process, we can conclude that a performance appraisal system can play a pivotal role in improving organisational performance, in general, and that of the T City Police, in particular.

(b) Research and experience have both shown that the successful implementation of performance appraisal systems is a difficult task. Many of the problems of implementation can be attributed to the frailties of the people who implement them – the problems arising from the subjective nature of assessment of performance being one of the most difficult of these.

In the case of the T City Police Force, the problems that are likely to arise stem from the restricted government funds available to the T City Police Force, the difficulties in setting realistic objectives for its police officers and from the problems that typically arise in using the appraisal system as the main basis for determining the level of PRPs.

Taking first the likely effect of restricted government funds, this is going to make the implementation of the appraisal and PRP system difficult in financial terms. The cost of training of large numbers of senior officers in appraisal will be expensive in terms of staff time. Once in place, the cost of conducting appraisals and the administration of the system all have to be accounted for. This time spent in these processes means that less time is available to be spent on law enforcement activity.

The second problem arising from the restrictions on government funding will occur when it comes to the point of allocating financial rewards to those who have met their appraisal objectives. If financial rewards in the form of PRP are relatively low or few in number, this will undermine their effectiveness as motivators and the police officers will lose confidence in the system.

Thirdly, one of the most frequently mentioned problems in the field of performance appraisal is that to do with the allocation of PRPs. The problem arises because of a tension which develops between the person conducting the appraisal and the person being appraised. During the appraisal, the manager, or in this case the senior police officer, is seeking to elicit full and frank disclosure from the person he is appraising with a view to offering assistance in training and development, or some other assistance. This problem of persuading individuals to admit their weakness during appraisal is difficult enough under ordinary circumstances but when the person doing the appraisal is also required to decide on levels of PRP, then the person being appraised becomes much less ready to admit to their weakness in case they spoil their chances of a merit increase. The whole basis of the appraisal is then under threat as the appraisal no longer provides the information required to meet the needs for which it was designed.

Finally, the problems entailed in the setting of objectives in police work can be formidable. In the case of the T City Police Force, the socio-economic conditions that generate crime are outside the control of individual officers. In these conditions, it does not make sense to set quantitative objectives because officers cannot fully determine their outcome. The problems involved in clearing up crimes vary enormously from one crime to another so it would be grossly unfair to allocate financial rewards on the basis of the number of crimes solved. The solving of many crimes also involves a great deal of teamwork and so any fair PRP system would have to develop a fair means of determining the contribution of individual officers. This would clearly be a very difficult task. It could be overcome by some kind of team-based PRP system but then the motivational effect for individuals would inevitably be reduced.

In these circumstances, other aspects of a police officer's performance could be measured such as their readiness to respond to emergency calls and the way they treat residents irrespective of race or creed. Performance-related payments could then be based on these qualitative measures. That said, it has to be admitted that these qualitative measures are more difficult to judge than quantitative measures and so are open to the kind of subjectivity that can undermine the trust of subordinates in the impartiality of the system.

Answer 2

(a) The implications for succession planning of the technological changes will be transformed from one that has concerned itself with grooming the trainee insurance professionals and sales personnel to fill posts left by retiring professionals, to one of training and developing and selecting a smaller number of able people to manage and administer what has become a more routine operation. With the fewer post-holders required for insurance professionals and more post-holders for the management of an increasing number of clerical level employees, F Company will need to adjust its succession plans to take account of the new senior positions within the company. Fewer senior insurance professionals will be required but possibly more managers of clerical and administrative staff, though this will depend, of course, on the effect that the new technology will have on productivity within the company and on the setting up of telephone call centres.

For individuals planning a career in the insurance industry, the simplification of the work, the reduced number of professional positions, and the associated insecurity of employment in the field will cause ambitious individuals to rethink their career plans. For the very ambitious, the restricted opportunities will present a challenge and require more careful planning than in the past as a means of gaining one of the fewer top jobs. For others, the new situation will cause them to consider entering another profession or line of work.

(b) The impact on the motivation of trainee insurance professionals and sales personnel is likely to be profound. Employees who entered the industry with the prospect of gaining professional status will see the chances of gaining entry to well-paid, high-status jobs diminishing and the real possibility of being forced to undertake a routine telesales or clerical job with diminished security of tenure facing them.

In terms of needs-based theories of motivation like those put forward by Maslow and Herzberg, it is evident that both the higher-level needs of recognition and self-actualisation, or sense of achievement, are unlikely to be met in the reorganised F Company. Not only that, but even some lower-level needs like those for security are less likely to be met than before the changes in organisation and staffing. The use of self-employed sales personnel means that F Company is less dependent on its own sales staff and so this, in turn, means less job security for its full-time sales staff.

In terms of expectancy theories of motivation, it is also apparent that the new situation is unlikely to motivate existing trainees. Their expectations will have been shattered by the changes that the new technology has brought to the industry. Instead of being encouraged to train and to develop the skills to become a fully fledged insurance professional or sales person, the trainee will come to doubt if the effort is worthwhile as the prospects of obtaining a professional position diminish.

Telephone call centres, by their very nature, provide limited opportunities for promotion to senior positions since most of the work is of a routine nature and requires only a limited number of personnel to manage the operation. The problem of keeping people motivated in such situations is, therefore, challenging.

Clerical jobs in telephone call centres have a reputation for routine repetitive work which can be tedious and boring. Psychologists have commented on the consequences for motivation of such routine unchallenging work. Maslow and Herzberg, in particular, have pointed out the need to provide work which is challenging and thus able to satisfy the higher-level psychological needs of people.

The extent to which people are bored at work is not due only to the nature of work itself. People differ in their response to work. Individual differences exist among people in terms of things like intelligence levels and other attributes. The effect of these differences is that, for some people, the repetitive forms of work are challenging enough. They are happy to have a predictable self-contained task that requires no special effort.

Some work is also so routine that it allows compensatory activities like daydreaming to be enjoyed. For many, however, the work in call centres is boring and monotonous and so there is a need to find ways of making the work tolerable and persuading those employed to give their best.

Many attempts have been made to redesign jobs to alleviate boredom and its more damaging consequences. These have included the rotation of jobs to introduce variety; for example job enrichment, which may involve the delegation of greater responsibilities to people, and the development of semi-autonomous groups/teams.

In the course of their efforts, researchers have found that the following characteristics of jobs appear to satisfy the social and psychological needs of employees:

- variety in tasks, and locations;
- autonomy in carrying out the task;
- a degree of responsibility for decisions about the job;
- a measure of challenge in the work, which leads to a sense of achievement on the completion of the job;
- the possibility for contact with others;
- task identity, which allows the recognition of work done and a sense of doing something worthwhile;
- clear objectives and feedback about performance to the jobholder.

To the extent that jobs in call centres can be organised in line with the above requirements, then motivation of staff should be assisted.

There are other ways to motivate personnel including the use of financial incentives, the use of an appropriate management style and ensuring fair and equal treatment for those employees who aspire to management positions within the organisation.

Answer 3

(a) We can classify the influences on ethical behaviour into those affecting the individual, those operating within the organisation and those influences in the organisation's environment that condition the ethical behaviour of those responsible for its management.

Individual ethical behaviour is influenced by family, religious values, personal standards and personal needs of various kinds. Research suggests that the early socialisation process is particularly important as early training and development have a strong influence on character development. Managers and staff who lack a strong and consistent set of personal values will find that their decisions vary from situation to situation as they strive to maximise their self-interests. In the case of corporations like *Enron* in 2002, it is evident that the self-interest of some senior management and some professional staff over-rode their commitment to acceptable standards of honesty and integrity. By contrast, people who operate within a strong ethical framework of personal rules or strategies will be more consistent and confident since choices are made against a stable set of ethical standards.

The organisation in which an individual is employed is also an important influence on ethical behaviour. Senior managers in their role as organisation leaders set the moral tone of the organisation through their example and through the system of rewards and punishments available to them. Similarly, the expectations and reinforcement provided by peers and group norms are likely to have a similar impact. Formal policy statements and written rules are also important in establishing an ethical climate for the organisation as a whole. They support and reinforce the organisational culture, which can have a strong influence on members' ethical behaviour.

Organisations operate in an environment composed of a wide variety of stakeholders including customers, suppliers, buyers, competitors, government, trades unions, political parties, pressure groups and local communities and are constrained by laws and regulations, and by social norms and values. These norms and values vary from society to society depending on historical and cultural heritage but, as countries become more integrated through the globalisation process, the business ethics acceptable in each country become more open to scrutiny and a convergence towards a common set of business ethics appears to be taking place.

The expectations of stakeholders play a key role in an organisation's ethical behaviour because if expectations are violated, then this will have repercussions that can affect the organisation's ability to operate. In the case of the US companies that violated the reporting standards expected of them, the companies were punished by legal penalties and by shareholders who sold their holdings.

(b) Formal codes of ethics are official written guidelines on how to behave in situations susceptible to the creation of ethical dilemmas. They have long been used in medicine, the law and other professions to regulate the ethical behaviour of their members and are now increasingly used in well-run organisations of all kinds.

These ethical codes try to ensure that individual behaviour is consistent with the values and shared norms of the profession or organisation. Codes of ethical conduct lay down guidelines on how to avoid illegal or unethical acts in the profession or job and on how employees should conduct themselves in relationships with clients and customers.

Areas frequently addressed include advice on bribes and kickbacks, political contributions, the honesty of records, customer–supplier relationships and the confidentiality of corporate information.

Useful though these codes are, they cannot cover all situations, and they cannot guarantee ethical conduct. The value of any formal code of ethics still rests on the underlying values of people recruited to the organisation, its managers and other employees. It is evident therefore that attention to recruitment and selection is important and that the criteria of selection should pay as much attention to the honesty and integrity of candidates as to their skills and abilities to perform the tasks and duties of the post they are recruited to.

Senior managers have the power to shape an organisation's policies and set its moral tone. They can and should serve as models of appropriate ethical behaviour for the entire organisation. Not only must their day-to-day behaviour be the example of high ethical conduct, but top managers must also communicate similar expectations throughout the organisation and reinforce positive results. The same responsibility extends to all managers in a position to influence the ethical behaviour of the people who work for and with them. Every manager becomes an ethical role model, and care must be taken to do so in a positive and informed manner.

A number of organisations now include some ethics training in their induction programmes. This is especially the case for UK pension providers and those involved in the selling of financial services more generally. A scandal of mis-selling and subsequent severe fines for the companies concerned has made them especially careful of the behaviour of the agents they now employ to sell their products.

Ethics training, in the form of structured programmes to help participants understand the ethical aspects of decision-making, can help people incorporate high ethical standards into their behaviours. Most ethics training is designed to help people deal with ethical issues while under pressure and to avoid the rationalisations for unethical behaviour that people are prone to indulge in to convince themselves that their unethical actions are justified.

One particular technique used in ethics training is worthy of special mention. This is the so-called mirror test in which trainees are confronted with the consequences of their behaviour if it should become widely known to the public.

The term "whistle blowers" refers to people who expose the misdeeds of others in organisations in order to preserve ethical standards and protect against harmful or illegal acts. While such behaviour does help to preserve ethical standards, it entails considerable risks for people who "blow the whistle". In many cases, exposure of misdeeds has damaging financial consequences for the organisations involved and damage to the reputation and careers of the people involved in the unethical behaviour. In such cases, the "whistle blowers" risk losing their present job and put their future career in jeopardy. It follows that if "whistle blowers" are to be encouraged to speak out, then appropriate legal protection must be available to prevent them suffering penalties for what is, in many ways, a public service.

Answer 4

(a) One theory of motivation often used to explain the adoption of financial incentive schemes like that operated by B plc is what Schein and others have called the "rational economic man theory". This theory assumes that people are motivated by self-interest and that the opportunity to accumulate significant sums of money will influence people to make additional efforts. The outcome of such extra effort by individuals, it is assumed, will benefit the whole organisation because productivity per head will increase and thus provide higher sales revenue with lower costs and higher profits.

The merits of the theory include its simplicity and its wide applicability in that entrepreneurs are ready to take considerable risks and expend great effort to develop profitable businesses, sales staff make great efforts to increase sales and production workers often rush around at speed in their efforts to gain bonuses paid for production of additional units.

The main limitation of the rational economic man theory, however, is that it is incomplete. In particular, it does not take account of the fact that people are motivated by factors other than money. The psychological theories of Maslow and Herzberg, for example, make clear that although money does play a role in motivating people to make extra efforts to gain additional income to satisfy basic needs, it is not the only incentive. Content theories of motivation like those of Maslow and Herzberg stress that once basic needs are satisfied, people are motivated by things like opportunities to gain status, recognition, a sense of achievement, a feeling of power and self-actualisation.

Money and wealth can, of course, act as a measure and a source of some of these rewards for effort, but the point is that many of these things that satisfy deeply felt psychological and social needs can be attained without money as an incentive.

Note: Other theories of motivation may be applied provided they offer an explanation of how financial incentives help to enhance employee performance.

(b) The merits of share incentive schemes, like the one operated by B plc, is that they do offer the opportunity for individuals who work for the company, a chance to benefit not only from the wages or salaries which they receive in return for their labour, but as shareholders to benefit from dividend income paid to shareholders as well as any increase in market value of their shareholding.

The main limitation of such schemes, however, is that the link is tenuous between effort expended and the increase in profits that bring dividend income and increase in share values. In other words, it is often difficult for a production worker to see a direct link between their own efforts and any increase in profits for a company because there are so many other factors that can affect profitability over which the individual worker has no control. For instance, employees might increase output and quality of their product only to find that the product does not sell because a competitor has introduced a better product, or is able to produce the same product at a lower price because of its acquisition of new technology, or a cheaper source of raw material supply or some other reason.

When profits begin to decline, as in the case of B plc, it is often the case that even though workers find themselves to be working harder than ever, the value of their shareholding continues to fall. In these situations, it is easy to see why some workers might conclude that the extra effort is not worthwhile because they are fighting a losing battle through no fault of their own.

Financial rewards could be more closely tied to the performance of employees by ensuring that employees have a high degree of control over the things they are measured on. In factory production, where the output of workers depends on their physical effort, performance is easier to measure than in much administrative, managerial and professional work, but even in this work it is possible to agree on approximate measures of performance on which payment can be based.

So any performance-related payment system that allows a direct link between the actual performance of the employee and the reward for that performance is more likely to motivate employees than in the case of the share scheme outlined in the question.

5

Change Management

Change Management

5

LEARNING OUTCOMES

By completing this chapter, including the readings and questions you should be assisted to:

- explain the process of organisational development;
- discuss how and why resistance to change develops within organisations;
- evaluate various means of introducing change;
- evaluate change processes within an organisation.

? Questions

5.1 The one thing that is known about change is that

A It is hard to manage
B It is always for the worse
C It is always an improvement
D It is ongoing and never ending

5.2 List each of Porter's Five Forces

(i)
(ii)
(iii)
(iv)
(v)

5.3 What are the main objectives of Organisational Development (OD)?

(i)
(ii)
(iii)
(iv)

5.4 What is a change agent?

A A close friend of James Bond
B Someone who gathers information on the competition
C A person (either internal or external) who facilitates change
D The person to blame when everything goes wrong

5.5 Explain the difference between planned change and emergent change.

5.6 Daft states that all of the following are needed for successful change except:

A Ideas
B Adoption
C Resources
D Results

5.7 What is the difference between:

(i) Incremental change
(ii) Step change
(iii) Transformational change

5.8 Kotter and Schlesinger identified six methods of dealing with resistance to change. These included all except:

A Education and communication
B Participation
C Negotiation
D Termination

5.9 What barriers do managers create for themselves when considering change?

5.10 Kurt Lewin suggested the Three-Stage Change Procedure. This included all the following except:

A Refreeze
B Defrost
C Unfreeze
D Change

5.11 Peter Drucker identified five basic rules to consider if acquisition is to be successful. These are

(i)
(ii)
(iii)
(iv)
(v)

5.12 Draw and label Greiner's growth model.

5.13 What alternative strategies might an organisation pursue other than growth?

5.14 Explain the meaning of:

(i) Unbundling
(ii) Downsizing
(iii) Rightsizing

5.15 What are the reasons Slatter identified for corporate decline?

5.16 Management can adopt a number of different approaches or styles when dealing with change. The four main ones are

(i)
(ii)
(iii)
(iv)

5.17 How did Senge define a Learning Organisation?

5.18 What is Kanter's prescription for encouraging organisational creativity?

5.19 What is the best-known model for monitoring changes in the external environment?

5.20 "T-groups" are used during the process of

A conflict management
B organisational development
C performance appraisal
D disciplinary proceedings

5.21 The view that "change is seen as continuous, unpredictable and open-ended" is known as

A emergent change
B planned change
C random change
D open change

5.22 Who introduced the concept of "thriving on chaos"?

A Kanter
B Senge
C Peters
D Lewin

5.23 What "can only be achieved by breaking with the traditional authoritarian, command and control hierarchy where the top thinks and local acts, to merge thinking and acting at all levels"?

A Motivation
B Theory E
C Theory O
D Organisational learning

5.24 In Greiner's growth model, which period tends to lead to a "crisis of red tape"?

A Growth through creativity
B Growth through collaboration
C Growth through delegation
D Growth through co-ordination

5.25 "I am just not interested" is an example of which form of resistance to change?

A Default
B Alienation
C Anxiety
D Ignorance

5.26 Which of the following is NOT a method of dealing with resistance to change, according to Kotter and Schlesinger?

A Education and communication
B Retirement and redundancy
C Manipulation and co-optation
D Explicit and implicit coercion

5.27 According to Daft, "uncertainty avoidance" is an example of

A a managerial barrier to change
B organisational development
C tacit acceptance of change
D the Abilene paradox

5.28 According to Lewin, "making the need for change so obvious that most people can readily understand it" is a definition of

A organisational learning
B unfreezing
C re-freezing
D education and communication

5.29 "Force field analysis" looks at

A the motivational aspects of change
B the forces driving, and restraining, change
C the forces of good and evil
D the use of explicit and implicit coercion

5.30 Third party consultants, therapy groups and confrontation are normally all associated with

A industrial disputes over terms and condition
B the process of job evaluation
C a firm experiencing severe trading difficulties
D organisational development (OD)

5.31 The most radical form of organisational change includes a cultural shift and is described as

A emergent change
B transformational change
C step change
D incremental change

5.32 Establishing a staff help line when attempting to cope with resistance to change is an example of

A facilitation
B manipulation
C coercion
D co-optation

Answers

5.1 D

5.2
(i) Industrial rivalry
(ii) Threat of new entrants
(iii) Threat of substitutes
(iv) Buyers bargaining power
(v) Suppliers bargaining power

5.3
(i) Increased level of trust amongst organisational members
(ii) Allowing problems to be addressed and solved
(iii) Enhanced and open communication
(iv) Increased individual and group problem-solving

5.4 C

5.5 *Planned*: Organisational change is seen as a process of moving from one fixed state to another via a series of pre-planned steps. Criticisms of this approach centre on issues of employee commitment and the rigidity of the approach.

Emergent: Based on the view that change is seen as continuous, unpredictable and open-ended, a process of constant adjustments. Emergent change emphasises a bottom-up approach where managers need to facilitate rather than make the change, making sure employees are receptive to changes and suitably skilled. Emergent approaches assume that organisations operate in unstable and/or unpredictable environments over which they exercise very little control. Change is, therefore, open-ended and ongoing, and emphasises employee flexibility, creation of cultures and structural adaptation. It requires genuine consultation, good communication and high levels of co-operation. It also implies a loss of managerial power and more trust in the individual worker which will not be acceptable to all organisations.

5.6 D

5.7 *Incremental change* has often comprised changes in response to trends in the environment such as sales growth or more commonly technological improvements. Usually, incremental change attempts to match organisational performance with the external environment, and gap analysis feeds back to corrective action. Where this is not seen, a "blinded" situation occurs which can lead to organisational decline.

Step change involves a situation where the trend line for a particular factor stops becoming smooth and there is a significant and unexpected jump in direction upwards or downwards.

Transformational change: Here radical change is involved and the organisation acts in a way that is currently outside of its existing paradigm (way of thinking). Clearly, this involves a huge cultural shift for this change to be brought about successfully.

5.8 D

5.9 Daft identified the following common problems for managers:

- excessive focus on costs
- failure to highlight benefits
- lack of co-ordination and co-operation
- uncertainty avoidance
- fear of loss.

5.10 B

5.11 (i) *Contribution*: The acquiring company must identify exactly what contribution it can make to the acquired company and this must be more than just money.

(ii) *Common core*: The companies involved should have some common core of unity in markets, production operations or technology.

(iii) *Value*: The company making the acquisition should value the products, services and customers of the other company.

(iv) *Management cover*: It is important that there is some top management cover available in case key senior managers in the acquired company choose to, or are required to, leave after the acquisition.

(v) *Linkage*: Within a year of the acquisition, managers should have been promoted across the boundaries of the two previously separate companies.

5.12

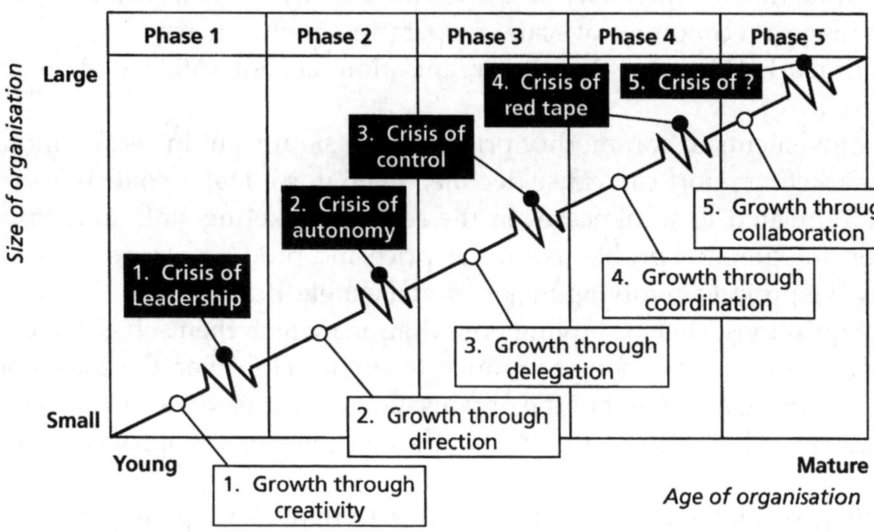

5.13 The strategic alternatives to growth include

- Maintain a status quo and ignore growth potential.
- Specialisation of the business, and building a future on distinct organisational competences.
- Innovation of products and markets.
- Divestment strategies, whereby parts of the business are closed or sold, usually as part of an attempt to consolidate or re-position the business.
- Reduction in geographical scope and/or product range.

5.14 (i) Unbundling is selling of parts of an organisation that no longer "fit" the strategic direction that the company wishes to move in. This frequently happens following an acquisition, as an organisation rationalises its new portfolio.

(ii) Downsizing is the phrase that is used to describe the action taken by an organisation when it reduces its workforce.

(iii) Rightsizing is similar to downsizing except that it implies that the organisation is restructuring to the "correct or right" size. Theoretically, this could include an increase in the workforce, but organisations usually rightsize in a downward direction.

5.15

Contributors to organisational decline
• Inadequate financial control, particularly when the management accounting systems are poorly designed, and/or management accounting information is not used by senior managers, and/or methods of overhead allocation distort costs.
• Poor management, typified by factors such as an overly autocratic chief executive, neglect of the organisation's core business and a weak board of directors.
• Competitive weaknesses due to products in decline and heavy emphasis on price competition.
• High cost structures, which may be the result of many factors, such as inability to take advantage of economies of scale or operating inefficiencies.
• Changes in market demand that the organisation has not anticipated and cannot respond to.
• Adverse movements in commodity prices can be significant in certain industries.
• Lack of marketing effort can cause decline; when it is a major contributory factor it is usually related to weaknesses in the senior marketing staff, and associated with other fundamental problems such as price and product competition.
• Too many big projects involving major capital expenditure.
• Unwise acquisitions, such as buying organisations which themselves have a weak competitive position, or paying too much for them. However, the most common problem is poor management of the organisation once it has been acquired.
• Poor financial policies, particularly overtrading and/or inappropriate financial sources.
• Overtrading, so that sales grow at a faster rate than the organisation is able to finance from its cash flow and borrowings.

Source: Slatter (1984)

5.16 (i) *The participative style*: Extensive delegation of tasks to teams and groups this requires time, trust and support.

(ii) *The interventionist style*: Limited delegation of some aspects of the change whilst retaining overall direction.

(iii) *The autocratic style*: No delegation direction is centrally driven.

(iv) *The educational style*: Facts are presented to staff and a rationale made for the change before change gets underway (a "tell and sell" approach).

5.17 Peter Senge has been one of the leading advocates of organisations developing the capacity and culture to become what he terms "learning organisations"; these are the ones that continually expand their ability to shape their future.

5.18 Kanter's prescriptions for encouraging organisational creativity are

- Develop an acceptance of change.
- Encourage new ideas at all levels of the organisation.
- Permit more interaction between individuals and groups.
- Tolerate failure, as experimentation requires trying out new ideas, not all of which will work.
- Offer recognition and rewards for creative behaviour.

5.19 A PEST or STEP analysis ideally linked to a SWOT analysis.

5.20 B

5.21 A

5.22 C

5.23 D

5.24 D

5.25 A

5.26 B

5.27 A

5.28 B

5.29 B

5.30 D

5.31 B

5.32 A

Section B questions

Question 1

X is a major car manufacturer, with a range of cars that are sold throughout the world. As the business environment of X has changed, the organisation has failed to change as much as its rivals. This has led to a situation where X's profits are falling and the directors are seriously concerned.

The HR director has suggested that X might benefit from a formal programme of organisational development (OD), but is unsure exactly what might be involved. The HR director is also concerned that production staff in X's two factories have always 'reacted badly' to any changes to their working routines. While each of the directors of X is very skilled and experienced in their own specialist area of the business, none has ever undertaken a major business change programme.

Requirements

(a) Identify Porter's five forces, and briefly explain how each of them might be a change trigger in the environment of X.

(5 marks)

(b) Explain the objectives of a formal organisational development (OD) programme.

(5 marks)

(c) Identify the aspects of X that are likely to be affected by a formal OD programme.

(5 marks)

(d) Discuss the responsibilities of a change agent in an OD programme.

(5 marks)

(e) Identify the competences necessary for any OD change agent to be successful.

(5 marks)

(f) Explain how Kotter and Schlesinger would suggest that X might overcome the resistance to change being exhibited by the production staff.

(5 marks)

(Total = 30 marks)

✓ Section B questions

Answer 1

(a) Porter's five forces are as follows:

1 Rivalry: Another car manufacturer might start to lower prices or introduce a new type of vehicle.
2 Bargaining power of suppliers: Manufacturers of, for example, tyres might increase prices
3 Bargaining power of buyers/customers: Customers might become more concerned with fuel economy or safety.
4 Threat of new entrants: X might find a car company from a previously "closed" economy, such as China, entering one of its markets.
5 Threat of substitutes: Rising fuel prices might lead to increased use of motorcycles or public transport.

(b) The objectives of a formal OD programme include the following:

- Increasing the level of trust among organisational members.
- Allowing problems to be confronted and solved by the people involved.
- Enhancing openness of communication between and within groups.
- Increasing the levels of individual and group responsibility for problem-solving and improvement.

(c) The aspects of X likely to be affected by a formal OD programme include the following:

- The organisational culture.
- The organisational climate.
- Employee commitment.
- Organisational conflict.
- Management development.

(d) The responsibilities of a change agent would include the following:

- To help the organisation to define the problem.
- To examine the causes of the problem, and diagnose how this might be overcome.
- To arrive at alternative solutions.
- To implement the chosen solution.
- To transmit the learning process to allow the organisation to deal with future change.

(e) The competencies required for a change agent to be successful include the following:

- Sensitivity to the goals of the organisation.
- Clarity of goal-setting.
- Flexibility in responding to change.
- Team-building.
- Networking.
- Tolerance of an uncertain environment.
- Communication skills.
- Interpersonal skills.

(There is a very long list of such competences in the CIMA learning system. Only 7 or 8 would be required.)

(f) Kotter and Schlesinger's suggestions for overcoming resistance to change are as follows:

- Education and communication: Explaining to the production staff why the change is necessary.
- Participation and involvement: Getting a production supervisor to project manage one aspect of the change.
- Facilitation and support: Appointing a counsellor, to hear staff issues.
- Negotiation and agreement: Offering a salary increase in return for co-operation.
- Manipulation and co-optation: Changing working practices, then recruiting some new staff to implement them.
- Explicit and implicit coercion: Making it clear that staff who do not comply will not be promoted.

Section C questions

Question 1

The DB Company operates in an expanding market. It has been unable to take advantage of its opportunities because of what appear to be problems of co-ordination within the company.

A representative of the DB Company has approached a firm of management consultants for advice on these problems and they have recommended the services of a specialist in Organisational Development (OD). The chief executive officer of the DB Company has never heard of OD and has asked for your advice.

Requirements

(a) Explain the nature of OD and describe how it might be used to assist the DB Company with the problems indicated in the scenario.

(16 marks)

(b) Describe the knowledge, skills and attitudes that the OD specialist would require, to take on the task of helping the DB company with its problems.

(14 marks)
(Total = 30 marks)

Question 2

The recently appointed Chief Executive Officer (CEO) of the F Steel Company is intent on making the organisation more competitive. He has made it clear that costs are too high and productivity too low. The trade union that represents the steel workers in the F Steel Company is well-organised and has promised the workers that it will defend their wage levels and working conditions.

The exchange rate of the local currency has been rising in value over the last year, and the company has to compete internationally with subsidised state steel companies. Though domestic demand for steel is weak, the market for steel in the Pacific Rim economies is still growing.

The company is suffering from a number of problems at the operational level. Deliveries have been late on a number of occasions and some customers have complained that the steel they have received does not match the agreed specification. Despite these problems, some of the F Steel Company's long-serving managers are complacent. They have seen the company come through many a business cycle and simply interpret the present situation as the trough of just another such cycle, which will pass. As a result, they see no need for any radical change.

Requirements

(a) Analyse the forces for change and causes of resistance in the F Steel Company. Classify these according to whether they can be considered as deriving from internal or external sources.

(12 marks)

(b) Recommend how the newly appointed CEO in the F Steel Company might go about managing the process of change.

(18 marks)
(Total = 30 marks)

Section C questions

Answer 1

(a) Organisational Development (OD) refers to the application of diagnostic and problem-solving skills by behavioural scientists to determine the nature of organisational problems and to a set of techniques to help overcome these.

Most OD specialists take a "systems" view of organisations. In other words, they conceive of an organisation as being made up of interdependent parts. From an OD perspective, the key aspect of a systems view is that organisational effectiveness depends on the optimum integration of the various parts so that all activities/functions work in harmony to produce organisational effectiveness.

The use of OD is most commonly called upon when a company faces severe problems as in the case of DB, but large, progressive organisations often retain OD specialists on their permanent staff to monitor operations and so prevent problems from arising.

The diagnostic phase of an OD programme usually begins with a review of the company's objectives and those of its sub-units. Particular attention will be given to the relationship between people; especially how well teams work together, the degree of collaboration between functional departments/divisions and leader–group relationships as well as the suitability of the organisation structure itself.

The techniques used in the diagnostic process are typically those of the questionnaire, interviews and observation. These are employed to build up a picture of staff attitudes and opinions as a means of identifying the basis of the company's problems.

Once the key problems have been identified, it will be necessary for the OD specialist to discuss with management the action required to solve the problems. This is a very important stage because success depends upon complete commitment from the senior management team. Such action may involve a re-alignment or re-ordering in the priority of the company objectives; changes to the structure of the organisation in whole or in part; re-allocation of responsibilities to different personnel and programmes of training.

Some of these action plans will be to do with changing the behaviour of staff members. OD specialists employ a range of techniques for this purpose. These include coaching and counselling, team-building activities, inter-group activities, role analysis, job redesign, planning and objective-setting activities and process consultation. This last technique, process consultation, is one in which the third-party consultant helps clients to see and understand the human processes that are taking place around them; for example, leadership issues, power struggles, communication problems and so on.

(b) Experience with OD programmes suggests that a particular combination of knowledge, skills and attitudes is necessary to be a competent OD specialist. These can be summarised as follows:

- In terms of knowledge, it is necessary that he/she possesses the requisite behavioural science background, and is experienced in the application of the diagnostic and problem-solving techniques detailed in *requirement* (a) above.
- The skills required are not only confined to those associated with the application of behavioural science knowledge, but also more general skills are needed such as interviewing skills, listening skills, presentation skills and the ability to establish and maintain working relationships with a wide cross section of people.

- Appropriate attitudes include a preference for interpersonal relations based on mutual trust and liking, for teamwork rather than competitiveness, and for conflict to be handled openly and constructively.

Answer 2

(a) One framework which can be used to analyse the forces for change and the resistance to change is K Lewin's "force field analysis". The forces for change and the origin of each of these in terms of internal or external sources are as follows:

Forces for change	*Origin*	
	Internal	*External*
Competitive pressures from other steel companies, particularly foreign-owned, state-subsidised companies		*
The exchange rate of the local currency that pushes up the price of steel to buyers from other countries		*
Lack of domestic demand, which puts pressure on costs and prices		*
Growing demand for steel in the Far East		*
Customer complaints about steel specification		*
Recently appointed CEO intent on making business more competitive	*	
Need for greater efficiency in organisation	*	

Forces resisting change	*Origin*	
	Internal	*External*
The attitude of the trade unions	*	
Complacency of long-serving managers	*	

(b) The most well used model in change management is probably that suggested by Lewin. (The use of other models, such as the Contingency model, is acceptable provided they are clearly described.) Lewin described his model as a form of "force field analysis". This involves identifying both the forces for change and the forces resisting change and estimating their relative strengths.

Once this analysis has been completed, Lewin argued that we need to seek ways to bolster any force that promote change in the direction we wish to move things, and to reduce any sources of resistance that may stand in the way of changes to be made.

Lewin recognised that some forces, particularly external forces, may well be outside management's control and so the concentration of management effort should be on internal forces for change and those factors or agents resisting them. Lewin's simple formula for tackling change consisted of a three-step process as follows:

- "Unfreezing" which involves reducing factors that maintain current behaviours and provide people with an understanding of why change needs to occur so that they can more easily accept it.

- Changing behaviour patterns in such a way that the new attitudes, values and behaviour are internalised as part of employees' new ways of thinking.
- "Refreezing" whereby supporting mechanisms are introduced to ensure that the new behaviour patterns are maintained such as reward systems and structures.

Applying this model to the situation faced by F Steel Company, we have to recognise that many of the forces acting upon the company are outside the control of the new CEO. There is little that can be done to manage these forces, except to join with other companies and lobby the government to assist the steel industry as a whole in some way. Such an effort may be directed to seeking to persuade the government to take action against imports of steel from state-subsidised, foreign steel companies and reducing the exchange rate of the country's currency.

Such efforts, however, are unlikely to bring results in the short term and so the CEO will need to focus on the forces over which he has more direct influence. In order to make changes that will increase its efficiency and effectiveness, the CEO can use the threat of competition to persuade employees, trade unions and long-serving managers that, unless changes are made, the very survival of the company and, therefore, the jobs of employees are in jeopardy. This reference to the threat of competition, accompanied perhaps by some action such as the introduction of a first round of redundancies, can act to unfreeze current attitudes and assumptions.

The next step of changing behaviour patterns, attitudes and beliefs is more difficult and will require a range of methods to persuade both managers and employees that change is necessary. Such methods will include ensuring that what needs to be changed and how it is to be effectively communicated, that all employees are involved in the change process through regular meetings and discussions, and that appropriate incentives and penalties are available to drive the changes.

Ideally, change is best achieved through willing participation of all concerned, but experience has taught us that resistance to change is common when the interests of individuals and groups are threatened. It will probably be necessary, therefore, for the CEO and his management team to negotiate changes with the trade unions. The threats to the company are so great, however, that the management can probably gain the trade unions' acceptance of the need for more efficient working practices and possibly a slimmer workforce.

Once these new working practices are in place, it is necessary according to Lewin's model that the new levels of efficiency are sustained and that management maintains a pressure for constant improvement to raise levels of productivity, so as to ensure continued survival of the business through rewarding desired behaviours.

6

Revision Questions

Revision Questions 6

Section A questions

Multiple choice questions

Question 1

1.1 The duplication of data in two or more files within a database is known as

A data warehousing
B data redundancy
C data integrity
D data backup

1.2 Which ONE of the following phrases explains "concentrated marketing"?

A The company produces one product for a number of different market segments
B The company introduces several versions of the product aimed at several market segments
C The company produces one product for a mass market
D The company produces one product for a single segment of the marketplace

1.3 An ABC system refers to

A a Japanese style problem-solving device that is particularly helpful in inventory management
B an inventory management method that concentrates effort on the most important items
C accuracy, brevity and clarity in the quality of system reporting
D a mainframe solution to managing inventory

1.4 When someone commences a new job, the process of familiarisation is known as

A Management development
B Recruitment
C Appraisal
D Induction

1.5 At what stage in Kurt Lewin's model of organisational change does the process of unfreezing take place?

A The termination stage
B The diagnostic stage
C The intervention stage
D The evaluation stage

1.6 When an organisation experiences sustained growth, this is often accompanied by

A Less structural rigidity
B A decrease in formal controls
C Higher debt
D An increase in formal rules and procedures

1.7 EFTPOS can be used to

A maintain stock records
B pay for goods
C market services
D locate stock items in a warehouse

1.8 The emphasis of "push promotion" is on

A ensuring that employees achieve their potential
B making consumers buy more
C persuading wholesalers and retailers to stock products
D making sure that customers are happy

1.9 Which of the following is NOT a classification of human behaviour, according to Schein?

A Self-actualising man
B Complex man
C Social man
D Emotional man

1.10 The motivating potential score, developed by Hackman and Oldham, is calculated to assess

A The knowledge of an individual
B The satisfaction with work
C The content of the job
D The quality of work performed

(Total = 20 marks)

Question 2

2.1 Which ONE of the following factors is most likely to lead to successful organisational change?

A Imposed by external consultants
B Maintaining existing policies and procedures
C Autocratic leadership
D Initiated and supported by top management

2.2 An assessment centre

A helps selection by assessing job candidates by using a comprehensive and interrelated series of techniques
B is the training headquarters where job interviews take place
C is a desk-based process of reviewing job application forms for suitability
D is a place where job applicants are subjected to psychological testing.

2.3 According to Douglas McGregor

A "Theory X" people dislike work, need direction and avoid responsibility
B "Theory Y" people dislike work, need direction and avoid responsibility
C self actualizing people dislike work, need direction and avoid responsibility
D hygiene factors determine whether people like work, need direction or take responsibility.

2.4 Effective product promotion is centred on

A production processes
B customers and communication
C bonuses for sales staff and product quality
D effective systems of monitoring and control.

2.5 Which ONE of the following is part of the recruitment, rather than the selection process?

A Job analysis
B Interviewing
C Testing
D Assessment centres

2.6 According to M A Devanna, which ONE of the following describes the components of the HR cycle?

A Job design, selection, involvement, appraisal, rewards
B Selection, performance, appraisal, rewards, development
C Performance, job design, appraisal, involvement, development
D Appraisal, development, job design, involvement, rewards

2.7 According to F W Taylor, which ONE of the following is a characteristic of scientific management?

A Work specialisation
B Group working
C Socio-technical system
D The informal organisation

2.8 The 5-S model refers to

A internal analysis involving structure, sub-structure, systems, sub-systems and strategy
B internal analysis involving style, shared values, skills, staffing and "soft" information
C operations management practices of structurise, systematise, sanitise, standardise and self-discipline
D the Japanese six-sigma model adapted to Western practice.

2.9 Planned organisational change is most commonly triggered by the need to respond to new threats or opportunities presented by

A The organisation's culture
B Developments in the external environment
C The internal environment
D Action by the organisation's management

2.10 Kaizen is a quality improvement technique that involves

A continuous improvement by small incremental steps
B a complete revision of all organisational processes and structures
C immediate, often radical "right first time" changes to practice
D a problem-solving fishbone technique to identify cause and effect.

(Total = 20 marks)

Question 3

3.1 Conventional marketing wisdom suggests that for successful segmentation of markets, segments must be

A relatively unsophisticated in their needs
B economic, efficient and effective
C measurable, accessible and substantial
D currently lacking in providers.

3.2 Gaining International Standards (ISO) in quality is mainly dependent upon

A effective processes for documentation and control
B a shared quality philosophy
C commitment from middle managers
D benchmarking customer-related performance against competitors.

3.3 The main advantage of a database is

A Data ownership
B Reduced data redundancy
C Reduced risk of failure
D Reduction in the volumes of paper records

3.4 Which ONE of the following statements regarding information is correct?

A Staff cannot have too much information whatever be the specific time period
B The structures should fit the information requirements of the organisation
C Information should flow vertically but not horizontally
D Information should flow horizontally but not vertically

3.5 In the process of HR planning, the first step is to

A assess the existing workforce
B forecast the potential supply of labour
C review the organisational mission, objectives and strategies
D forecast HR needs

3.6 An individual can be said to have reached a career plateau when

A Promotions cease
B Promotions decrease
C Demotion takes place
D Promotions increase

3.7 Kurt Lewin's ideas on change are based on the view that change is

A capable of being planned
B emergent
C inevitable and uncontrollable
D transformational.

3.8 Attempts to secretly influence others by offering only selective information is a means of dealing with resistance by

A Participation
B Force coercion
C Facilitation
D Manipulation and co-option

3.9 In Frederick Herzberg's two-factor theory of motivation, base pay is considered to be what kind of factor?

A Motivator
B Hygiene
C Equity
D Valence

3.10 Distribution channels, transport, warehouse and sales outlet locations are all examples of

A "place", one component of the marketing mix
B "promotion", one component of the marketing mix
C "physical evidence", one component of the marketing mix
D the management of operations for a service organisation.

(Total = 20 marks)

Question 4

4.1 Adding new tasks to a person's job, so increasing their responsibility, is called

A process re-engineering
B job enrichment
C HR development
D career scoping.

4.2 Frederick Herzberg's study of work and people is of significance to managers because it identifies

A a framework for HRM involving appraisal, training and motivation
B the need to assess the personality of job applicants
C factors associated with job satisfaction called motivators
D satisfaction from a participative, problem solving environment.

4.3 Job family structures are examples of

A motivational tools
B similar levels of responsibility reflected across several distinct functions or disciplines
C Japanese employment practice
D pay structures for jobs within distinct functions or disciplines.

4.4 The intervention of a consultant or change agent is a common feature of

A co-operation and negotiation strategies for change
B an inclusive culture
C high levels of management visibility
D a programme of Organisational Development (OD).

4.5 Data redundancy arises as a result of

A viruses and computer misuse
B downsizing the organisation
C a lack of password controls
D duplication of data held.

4.6 The set of activities designed to familiarise a new employee with an organisation is called

A job analysis
B induction
C selection
D manipulation and co-optation.

4.7 Public relations activity can be used within marketing as part of

A marketing decision support activities
B a promotional mix
C customer feedback processes
D segmentation practices.

4.8 Recruitment involves

A advertising a vacancy and interviewing
B conducting interviews and tests
C advertising a vacancy and initial screening of candidates
D ensuring that contract negotiation complies with organisational policy.

4.9 Remuneration is an example of

A self-actualisation reward
B an intrinsic reward
C an extrinsic reward
D an individual's work/life balance.

4.10 The purpose of a person specification is to provide details of

A organisational size and diversity of activity
B the types of responsibilities and duties to be undertaken by the post holder
C personal characteristics, experience and qualifications expected of a candidate
D individual terms of engagement and period of contract.

(Total = 20 marks)

✓ Multiple choice solutions

Answer 1

1.1 B
1.2 D
1.3 B
1.4 D
1.5 C
1.6 D
1.7 B
1.8 C
1.9 D
1.10 C

Answer 2

2.1 D
2.2 A
2.3 A
2.4 B
2.5 A
2.6 B
2.7 A
2.8 C
2.9 B
2.10 A

Answer 3

3.1 C
3.2 A
3.3 B
3.4 B
3.5 C
3.6 A
3.7 A
3.8 D
3.9 B
3.10 A

Answer 4

4.1 B
4.2 C
4.3 D
4.4 D
4.5 D
4.6 B
4.7 B
4.8 C
4.9 C
4.10 C

? Objective test questions

Question 1

Each of the sub-questions 1.1 to 1.5 below requires a brief written response.
Each sub-question is worth 4 marks. This response should be in note form and should not exceed **50** words per sub-question.

1.1 Describe the relationship between operations management and (using Mintzberg's terminology) the organisational technostructure.

(4 marks)

1.2 Explain how continuous inventory systems might work against an organisation's Just-in-Time (JIT) philosophy.

(4 marks)

1.3 Identify examples of external failure costs, and explain their significance for an organisation with a reputation for quality.

(4 marks)

1.4 Distinguish between push and pull marketing policies and their impact on the promotion of goods.

(4 marks)

1.5 Identify the main stages involved in developing human resource plans and programmes following the production of a corporate plan.

(4 marks)
(Total = 20 marks)

Question 2

Each of the sub-questions 2.1 to 2.5 below requires a brief written response.
Each sub-question is worth 4 marks. This response should be in note form and should not exceed **50** words per sub-question.

2.1 Explain the relationship between "data independence" and a database approach to flexible data management.

(4 marks)

2.2 Briefly explain the main factors management should take into account when choosing computer hardware.

(4 marks)

2.3 Describe the ways in which Total Productive Maintenance might contribute towards a manufacturing organisation's quality programme.

(4 marks)

2.4 Distinguish Quality Assurance (QA) systems from quality control systems.

(4 marks)

2.5 Compare and contrast product-orientated organisations and production-orientated organisations.

(4 marks)
(Total = 20 marks)

Question 3

> Each of the sub-questions numbered 3.1 to 3.5 below requires a brief written response. Each sub-question is worth 4 marks.
>
> This response should be in note form and should not exceed **50** words per sub-question.

3.1 Explain the concept of physical evidence when applied to the marketing mix.

(4 marks)

3.2 Identify the potential benefits of a marketing database and the source data from which it might be constructed.

(4 marks)

3.3 In HR planning how might an organisation match the projected "supply" of human resources to future demand.

(4 marks)

3.4 Identify the advantages and disadvantages of a policy of succession planning for a large organisation.

(4 marks)

3.5 Identify both the advantages and disadvantages of a decentralised Human Resource provision for an organisation that has many business units and sites.

(4 marks)
(Total = 20 marks)

Objective test answers

Answer 1

1.1 The relationship between operations management and the organisational technostructure.

Operations management

- Developing outputs (products/services) by transforming inputs (stock, human) through operations (manufacturing, assembly and so on).

Technostructure

- Expert advice, training, research, standardising processes, outputs and skills.
- Involves work-study, HR managers and so on.

Relationship: OM = operating core and finances a technostructure that helps make operations effective.

Note to readers: In larger organisations, some parts of the technostructure may devote themselves to operations management issues alone.

1.2 Continuous inventory systems working against a JIT philosophy.

Continuous inventory

- Monitoring to keep above a predetermined level.
- Fixed amount ordered.
- Zero demand buffer stocks ("just in case"); inconsistent with JIT.

JIT philosophy (eliminate all waste; right part at the right place at the right time) better supported with JIT inventory approach.

1.3 The type and significance of external failure costs for an organisation with a reputation for quality.

External failure = costs of substandard goods sold, for example:

- "Free" replacement.
- Redesign/rework costs, wastage and so on.
- Warranty claims.
- Product liability and damages

Significance = Goods with customer, meaning:

- Damaged reputation/staff morale?
- Loss of repeat sales/future custom?
- Reduced customer confidence?
- Bad PR (complaints).

1.4 Push and pull marketing policies and their impact on the promotion of goods.

Firms may have:

- Suppliers (downstream)
- Supply others (upstream)

in a value chain that links to ultimate consumer.

	"push"	*"pull"*
Aim	"push" to wholesalers/retailers who sell to customers.	Influence final consumers' attitudes through for example advertising. Consumer demand "pulls" through.
Promotion to consumer	Final firm in value chain.	Shared by manufacturer.

1.5 Main stages in developing HR plans and programmes following production of a corporate plan.

Stages:

1 A supply forecast

- Analysis of existing resources.
- Projection of likely changes over period (natural wastage, turnover and so on.).

2 Identify demand implied by corporate plan.
3 Articulate both forecasts in HR plan.
4 Develop programmes with target dates to reconcile supply and demand. (Address recruitment, selection, training, management development, transfers, redeployment, redundancies and so on.)

Note: This explanation is based on Mullins (2005). It is not the only way of understanding the stages. Other thinkers may express a need for internal and external data collection and analysis using models such as PESTLE and so on. Valid alternative approaches to that suggested by Mullins also received credit.

Answer 2

2.1 A database approach involves collecting integrated common data that is then shared throughout the organisation.

Data independence is an essential feature of a database approach. It means that data exists independently of the programs that use it. This gives increased flexibility.

2.2 Main factors when choosing computer hardware include:

- Suitability: Cost, user requirements
- Acceptability: Manufacturer's reputation, computer specification, built in features (for example security)
- Feasibility: Compatibility with existing systems, computers used elsewhere within the organisation's industry and so on.

2.3 Total productive maintenance plans and implements the systematic maintenance of all equipment. This increases productivity and prevents unplanned breakdowns.

- Helps consistent production.
- Reduces scrap and rework so lowering cost of quality.
- Improves accuracy of forecasting requirements.
- Staff morale improved as quality increases.

2.4 Quality Control (QC) systems attempt to **control** quality whereas

Quality Assurance (QA) systems attempt to **create** quality

QC involves managing each stage of production to minimise errors (a third party, negative intervention process). QC inspects afterwards.

QA checks quality in a positive way encouraging worker ownership for quality and "zero defects".

2.5

	Product orientated	*Production orientated*
Main focus	Product features	Production efficiency
Quality	May be high	May be low
Cost	May be high	Low
Sales	Not sufficiently considered	Low quality may lead to lower sales

Neither organisation:

- Has researched market demand
- Is in touch with customers and their requirements

Both risk products not selling sufficiently.

Note: An alternative valid interpretation of the organisations could be as follows:

Production-orientated companies have a production department budget (excluding purchasing) representing the largest percentage of company turnover, for example Rolls Royce, whereas a product-orientated company is one where the design department budget represents the largest proportion of turnover, for example Amstrad E phones.

Answer 3

3.1 Marketing mix = a manufacturing firm's "blend" of price, product, promotion, place

For Service organisations other relevant factors include a lack of "physical evidence" because:

- Services are intangible
- Potential customers may therefore feel greater risk

Reassurance is therefore needed, for example testimonials/references from past customers.

Note: Other examples apart from testimonials/references might be given such as internet pages, paperwork, brochures, uniforms, the corporate logo, buildings, furnishings and signage etc.

3.2

Sources	*Benefits*
One-off market research data already available	Improves problem solving capacity
Other marketing intelligence	Method of structuring decisions
Internal information on products, trends, markets and competitors, etc.	Integrates all types of knowledge
	Maximises IT potential
	Total system of marketing information to support decisions

3.3 HR planning: satisfying projected demand by adjusting projected "supply".

Increasing	*Reducing*
Re-training/re-skilling/multi-ski I ling for potential "gaps"	Early retirements
Development for internal promotions (succession planning)	Redundancy
Overtime	Short-time working
Increased use of IT	Job-sharing
Outsourcing	
Recruitment and selection (new employees)	
Internal transfers/re-deployment to balance requirements	

3.4

Advantages	*Disadvantages*
Career structures, rewards visible	Lack of exposure to other influences
Positive motivation	Ignores possible better candidate from outside
Reinforces existing culture	Trend for movement between companies strong
Rational approach	Vacancies may arise at inconvenient times
	Expensive (?)
	Needs managing
	Only possible within a very large organisation
	Outdated concept?

3.5

Advantages	*Disadvantages*
Empowerment/delegation strengthened	Lack of central control
In touch with detained unit/site issues	Lack of specialist knowledge
Greater local knowledge	May lead to "maverick" actions/policies
Visible	HR function may be diluted
	Uneven provision within organisation

? Section B questions

Question 1

The country of Chapterland has a principle that healthcare should be free to its citizens at the point of access. Healthcare is funded from national taxation and organised through a series of large health units, one of which is known as "Q2". Q2 operates a huge, single site hospital and offers a variety of community services (such as health visiting) that are taken to the local population. Q2 has a management structure consisting of eight clinical and administrative directors who report to Q2's Chief Executive Officer (CEO). The Q2 CEO is directly accountable to the national government through regular returns of information and year-end reporting.

Published "quality league tables" of hospital performance against government targets suggest that Q2 has one of the worst records in the country. (Targets are for cleanliness of hospital wards, treatment waiting times and staff employed per patient cases dealt with.) In addition, Q2 has in recent years been operating to a budget in excess of its funding, which is against government regulations. The current year budget again exceeds projected funding.

Last year, Q2's previous CEO decided that certain changes were necessary including:

- better cost control;
- improved performance measurement; and
- benchmarking.

He revealed this thinking for the first time in a global email he sent to Q2's staff. Later, when conducting the annual performance appraisal of the Director of Human Resources (HR), he tasked her with implementing "each and every form of benchmarking" within the next 4 months so that "true" performance deficiencies could be addressed. However, the Director of HR left for a new job elsewhere within that period. The CEO then undertook to manage the changes himself but was surprised to find directors unenthusiastic and even uncooperative. Under pressure from the government the CEO resigned "for personal reasons" and no progress was made with his initiatives.

A new CEO has just been appointed. Her immediate concern is to reduce expenditure and improve performance. On her first day as CEO she spoke of a need to re-establish a culture of "care through quality" within Q2. She wishes to discuss a number of ideas and issues with her clinical and administrative directors at a special "away day" meeting to be arranged soon. You work in the CEO's central policy team and she has informed you that some ideas for initiatives include outsourcing, improved supply management and new performance management measures.

Requirements

You have been asked to provide the new CEO with briefing notes on a number of issues that will help prepare her for the "away day" meeting. These notes should:

(a) Explain why the changes attempted by the previous CEO were unsuccessful.

(5 marks)

(b) Explain the role Human Resources could perform in supporting any new initiatives for change.

(5 marks)

(c) Analyse the potential of outsourcing as a means of overcoming some of the problems facing Q2. (The CEO has identified two services initially; IT/IS and cleaning.).

(5 marks)

(d) Discuss which forms of benchmarking Q2 should use in order to contribute to better performance management.

(5 marks)

(e) Discuss how a culture of "care through quality" might be established within Q2.

(5 marks)

(f) Describe the performance measures that will be needed in order to satisfy future management and strategic reporting requirements of Q2.

(5 marks)

(Total = 30 marks)

Important note: Use a separate page of your answer book for each sub-question. You should limit your answer for each sub-question to no more than one page.

Question 2

S & C is a medium-sized firm that is experiencing rapid growth evidenced by increased turnover. It has been able to develop a range of new consultancy and specialist business advisory services that it offers to its growing customer base. To cope with these developments several organisation-wide initiatives have been launched over the past 2 years.

The existing financial systems are struggling to cope with these developments, but replacement software is due to be installed within the next 6 months. The new system was justified partly because it could reduce costs although precise details have not been given. The application software does not fit existing business processes exactly. However, it has the clear advantage of giving S & C access to an industry best practice system and is identical to that used by all its main competitors and some of its clients.

A three-person project steering group has recommended that a phased approach to introduction should be used and has undertaken most of the project planning. A programme of events for implementing the system has been agreed but is not yet fully operational. This group has not met for a while because the designated project manager has been absent from work through illness.

You are Head of S & C's Central Support Unit. You also serve on the project steering group.

A partners' meeting is due to take place soon. The firm's senior partner has asked you to prepare a PowerPoint presentation to other partners on implementation issues. You understand that partners are conscious that system implementation represents a form of further organisational change. They are asking questions about the approach that will be taken to the introduction of the new system, likely changes to practices, critical areas for success, system testing, support after implementation, system effectiveness and so on.

Requirements

You are required to produce outline notes that will support your eventual PowerPoint presentation. These notes should:

(a) Discuss the options to overcome the fact that the software does not fit existing business processes exactly.

(5 marks)

(b) Explain why a phased approach to introducing the system is, in this case, more suitable than a direct "big bang" approach.

(5 marks)

(c) Discuss the ways in which particular individuals and groups within S & C are important for implementation to succeed.

(5 marks)

(d) Explain how users should be involved in the implementation phase of the project.

(5 marks)

(e) Describe the training that should be given to targeted groups within S & C.

(5 marks)

(f) Explain the aims of a post-implementation review.

(5 marks)

(Total = 30 marks)

Important note: Use a separate page of your answer book for each sub-question. You should limit your answer to each sub-question to no more than one page.

✓ Section B answers

Answer 1

Requirement (a)

Why the changes attempted by the previous CEO were unsuccessful,

A number of mistakes were evident in the management of the changes;

Lack of consultation

The CEO rightly decided that certain key changes were necessary. Although he may have been correct in identifying the areas he did, there is no suggestion that he consulted on the required key changes. As a result, there is no certainty that these initiatives alone would bring about the desired changes. The changes needed may have involved a need for cultural change, which appears to have been ignored.

Lack of two way communication and ownership

The CEO revealed his thinking for the first time in a global email sent to Q2's staff. It may have been advisable to use these thoughts as a basis for discussion and involve staff in order to:

- raise awareness of the issues
- generate new thinking and ideas
- take ownership of the change initiatives

Not taking responsibility for the change

The use of the annual performance appraisal process to delegate responsibility for the changes was not advisable. Further, it is debateable whether the Director of HR should have been made responsible for it. It could be seen that the CEO abdicated responsibility rather than assuming a role of a visible driving force in the early stages. For such important developments, the CEO or perhaps some management consultant may have been more appropriate to lead the change programme. When the Director of Human Resources left for a new job elsewhere, the CEO became the change agent himself. This meant that the impetus for change had been lost. The Chief Executive Officer's subsequent resignation meant that two change agents had been unsuccessfully used.

Lack of involvement of clinical and administrative directors

Directors other than the Director of HR may have felt excluded from the process (hence their apparent lack of enthusiasm and cooperation). It would have been advisable to discuss matters with them initially before all staff were communicated with. They may have felt undervalued and also felt that their authority had been undermined.

Inappropriate communication method

Using email to inform staff of such important changes is inappropriate for communicating a change of this magnitude. Email is impersonal and it is unlikely that every member of staff would be able to access this medium. Email is in any case best for quick factual information sharing only.

Faulty planning

There is no evidence of

- how cost control might be improved
- specific plans for how changes were to be implemented
- allocations of extra time and resources
- sensitivity as to how the changes would affect staff.

Requirement (d)

The role Human Resources could perform in supporting any new initiatives for change. The role identified by the previous CEO for the Director of HR took insufficient account of the potential contribution that the HR function can make to organisational change (See (a) earlier). Human Resource Management (HRM) involves the following:

- A strategic approach.
- Acquisition, motivation, development and management of the organisation's human resources.
- Helping to achieve corporate performance through people.
- An alignment of HR practices to corporate strategies,
- The use of HR specialists to help organisational controllers (in this case directors and managers within directorates) to meet management objectives.

Within this context HR could properly help support the new initiatives for change through:

- Discussion of the proposed initiatives and a contribution to their formulation in conjunction with other professional and clinical groups.
- Obtaining intelligence on HR practices used in other health units that appear to be performing better than Q2.
- Developing HR practices that will support the agreed initiatives (for example identifying expertise necessary to make the changes, new skill requirements, the appropriateness of reward packages that will support implementation of changes, liaison with staff and trade unions groups and so on).
- Identifying, then arranging for, HR actions to support the initiatives specifically staff training, a different emphasis when recruiting, and performance measures and bonuses to encourage quality and cost control.
- Considering the changes required to the Q2 culture and ways of achieving these.
- Constant support, counselling, coaching and communication with those individuals identified as key in bringing about the necessary changes.
- Developing appropriate HR monitoring and control mechanisms that will support the initiatives.

Requirement (c)

Outsourcing as a means of overcoming some of the problems facing Q2. (Initially: IT/IS and cleaning.)

Problems facing Q2

- Expenditure in excess of funding.
- A relative failing in terms of government targets on cleanliness, waiting times and staffing levels. Government and the new CEO apparently interpret this as indicating "poor quality".

About outsourcing

Involves contracting out non-core services to specialist providers rather than attempting to provide them in-house. Consistent with a "stick-to-your-knitting" concept, in this case providing health care not those things that support it.

Some issues

All organisations view outsourcing differently (for example hostile, apathetic, a necessary evil, a positive development and so on). If outsourcing is not viewed favourably there is likely to be strong resistance to the proposal. There is no indication how Q2 feels but it may be counter productive if there is likely to be strong staff and union resistance.

- Unclear why information services and cleaning have been chosen as pilots: possible staffing/resourcing difficulties?
- What is the experience of other health units?

Advantages of outsourcing

- Helps numerical flexibility and should improve performance against government target on staff employed per patient cases.
- May reduce costs initially (but debatable if it will improve quality performance).

Disadvantages of outsourcing

- Potential lack of understanding of health service ethos by contractors of the outsourced service.
- May not contribute positively to culture of "care through quality".
- Additional cost associated with determining service specifications, and ultimately monitoring performance.
- Q2 is already under performing in cleaning: will outsourcing make it worse?
- Possible resistance from unions representing in-house service workers who will lose their jobs within Q2.

Summary

It is unclear how the outsourcing of these services (particularly IT) can directly contribute to solving Q2's problems.

If there is likely to be low resistance to the initiative it could be seen as a good idea for the following reasons:

- It indicates to government that something is being done.
- Short term "hit" against government targets of staff employed per patient cases dealt with.

The initiative's contribution to the more enduring goal of "care through quality" is more uncertain.

Requirement (d)

Benchmarking Q2 should use in order to contribute to better performance management.

Benchmarking is:

- a process of systematic comparison of a service, practice or process against one or more similar activities;
- a contributor to continuous improvement in the levels of performance;

- a means of identifying good/best practice which could lead to an understanding of how this has been achieved and therefore how Q2 might improve;
- a means of overcoming inertia and driving organisational change.

Relationship to performance management:

- concentrates on performance and value-adding processes;
- improves management's understanding of Q2:s relative strengths and weaknesses;
- helps shape a culture of striving for "best in class";
- provides advance warning of deteriorating performance;
- establishes key information that management can use to exercise control and make effective decisions.

Main types of benchmarking:

Internal benchmarking: based on the notion that there are performance differences *within* the organisation itself (these may be as a result of geographical differences, history, customs, working relationships and so on). As Q2 is a single site hospital, it is unlikely that internal benchmarking will be of much value.

Competitive benchmarking: comparison of various activities with those of competitors. Q2 needs to identify a similar hospital to compare itself with. This may be rather easier within the public sector than in the private sector where details of profits and processes are kept as secret as possible. Published "league tables" of hospital performance are an existing form of competitive benchmarking but are restricted to cleanliness; treatment waiting times and staff employed per patient cases. The government may have other comparator ratios readily available (based on annual returns) and is likely to be sympathetic to letting Q2 use them in this way.

Best practice activity benchmarking: the identification of state-of-the-art products, services or processes of any relevant organisation (not necessarily in healthcare). The objective is to identify best practice in any type of organisation that has established a reputation for excellence in specific business activities. (This might be in catering, telephone response times, IT or other support services.)

In summary, aspects of benchmarking for Q2 to progress:

Priority 1: Competitive benchmarking against performance of other health units.

Priority 2: Best practice where relevant comparator established.

Requirement (e)

How a culture of "care through quality" might be established within Q2.

On her first day the new CEO spoke of a need to re-establish a culture of "care through quality".

The implications of this are as follows:

- To improve healthcare, Q2 needs to improve quality in everything it does.
- This implies a shared philosophy (as part of a cultural understanding) rather than an accreditation process, namely, a total quality management (TQM) approach to quality
- The use of the phrase "re-establish" suggests that this was once present in Q2 but there has been some drift. The philosophy will not be alien to Q2 staff but will mean a return to past core values. This suggests that there will be little cultural resistance.

TQM as a way of achieving "care through quality" means:

- An integrated, comprehensive system of planning and controlling all business functions.
- A philosophy of business behaviour embracing principles such as employee involvement, continuous improvement at all levels and customer focus, as well as being a collection of related techniques aimed at improving quality such as full documentation of activities, clear goal setting and performance measurement from the customer perspective.

How this might be established within Q2:

Developing a commitment to quality at all levels in Q2 and a focus on continuous improvement (Kaizen) of everything however small. (Kaizen involves the continual analysis of organisational processes to ensure continued improvement in performance and quality.)

- Re-establishing a widespread commitment to quality improvement amongst staff and those contracted to work on behalf of Q2 through improved communication.
- Focusing on patients, local citizens and government as Q2's customers.
- Strengthening working relationships between all clinical and administrative directorates and the building of multi-functional teams.
- Involvement of all in discussing and measuring quality, including setting of standards and gathering information.
- Establishing relevant review, feedback and appraisal processes to find ways of doing things better.
- Investing in systems that will provide relevant timely information and the establishment of regular reporting of key indicators of quality.
- A realignment of reward and incentive systems to positively encourage quality.
- Training in areas where Q2 is felt to be weak. Quality can only be achieved by competence in whatever job or activity is undertaken.
- The establishment of quality circles and project teams to bring about positive change.

Requirement (f)

Performance measures needed in order to satisfy future management and strategic reporting requirements of Q2.

Q2 needs to develop an integrated package of performance measures that will support future performance management. These will need to incorporate:

Management

- Data required by government in the compilation of its league tables. Targets are currently for cleanliness of hospital wards, treatment waiting times and staff employed per patient cases dealt with. More information may be needed in the future as a result of government decisions. Good practice suggests that this data converted into ratios and so on would also be useful to management in interpreting, monitoring and controlling performance.
- Year-end returns including budgetary performance. This also is a requirement when reporting to government
- Data required as a result of decisions on benchmarking,
- Data required in support of TQM initiatives and other continuous improvement measures will need to be established and gathered. Historical trends can then be produced that should identify improvement over time.
- Information on financial aspects of the operation including costs, performance against budgets, activity-based costing and soon. Overall financial performance is a concern,

and management accounting has a significant role to play in developing relevant measures. Appropriate management accounting information (such as costs per medical procedure) might usefully be progressed.

Strategic

In addition Q2 may wish to develop further measures of performance that will require data of a quantitative and qualitative nature for instance:

- A balanced scorecard, a strategic approach to performance measurement incorporating measures within four dimensions: financial, customer, internal and business, and innovation and learning.
- Value For Money (VFM) measures aimed at gauging overall economy, efficiency and effectiveness in the use of resources in the absence of a profit measure.

Answer 2

Requirement (a)

Options to overcome the software not fitting the existing business processes exactly.

Change will be required as a result of the mismatch between the software and the existing business processes. There appear to be two distinct options:

Option 1. Change the software.

Option 2. Change the business processes.

The choice should be made taking account of all relevant costs and benefits and might be made using suitable evaluation criteria such as suitability, acceptability and feasibility (or similar). The applications software is designed to perform specific financial functions of the business. It is essentially an "off the shelf" rather than a bespoke solution but could conceivably be adapted. Such an adaptation could be financially costly. There is also a need to identify the necessary expertise to carry out this software development and the company may need to employ an outside source for the purpose.

Changing the business processes represents yet another change initiative that staff may respond to negatively. As competitors and peers are using the software already it is reasonable to assume that it will encapsulate industry best practice. These organisations apparently operate in that way that is consistent with the software. This implies that S & C may operate in an inconsistent and possibly inefficient fashion.

Requirement (b)

A phased approach: particularly more suitable than a more direct "big bang" approach.

The more direct "big bang" approach generally represents the highest risk, as at a predetermined point in time the old system ceases to operate completely. Using this approach there is no opportunity to validate the new system's output with the old, so management must have complete confidence in the new system. As the software in question appears to be something of an industry standard there is likely to be some general confidence in it. However, there appears to be something of a mismatch between the system and corresponding processes, which could prove a difficulty.

The phased approach involves gradual implementation possibly involving one subsystem at a time. This might involve implementing the system by first converting the customer accounts subsystem, then the reporting subsystem and so on. This offers distinct advantages in this particular case:

- Staff is likely to be suffering "change fatigue" from previous initiatives and can only endure so much upheaval while continuing to function effectively.
- The continued support of the partners as project sponsors is important and they are likely to see "deliverables" sooner with a phased roll-out.
- The phased approach is less risky given that the project manager could be unavailable to oversee the change.
- The project management risk (heightened by the absence of the project manager) will be reduced as issues found in small-scale use of the new system can be remedied in time for wider software roll-out.

Requirement (c)

The ways in which particular individuals and groups within S & C are important for implementation to succeed

- *Partners.* Support from the top is crucial. They must visibly support the implementation.
- *Users.* Successful user acceptance and buy-in is also key as they are the main recipients of the change. Meaningful communication is necessary, also participation to get commitment through joint analysis of issues to engender feelings of "ownership".
- *The users' managers.* These managers will be called upon to help ensure that disruptions are kept to a minimum during and immediately after changeover. Communication and involvement again is necessary (albeit to a different degree to users).
- *Project manager.* Effective project management is crucial to ensure that S & C's corporate performance does not falter. The project manager has been absent with illness and matters cannot be allowed to "drift". If the illness is long term a replacement project manager needs to be appointed swiftly.
- *Those in the HR Department.* If system success depends on people behaving in certain ways (for example sharing information across departments, taking greater responsibility and so on) reward systems may need to be adjusted possibly including new incentives, metrics and evaluation criteria. Effective training programmes will also be needed. Formal policies and structures may also need adjustment.
- *Project steering group.* Needs to address the real sources of resistance to change and means of overcoming them. Proposals are also needed in order to successfully align financial systems and business processes. (It is important that some members of the group are available in the weeks after going live to answer questions and give support to users).

Requirement (d)

Users involvement in testing the system during the implementation phase

As mentioned earlier user acceptance is vital. It is also important to test the system during the implementation phase. It is a good idea to combine these two requirements.

Users might be usefully involved in a number of ways and could be used to:

- Act as guinea pigs for any system developments through testing in association with the new procedures and processes.

- Contribute to quality circles and discussion forums.
- Assess the effectiveness of training programmes, etc. and provide feedback.
- Provide mutual mentoring/assistance/"buddying" to other new users of the system.
- Collect data on the costs and benefits of the overall business change, not just the software application.
- Be involved and act as advocates of change to colleagues.

Requirement (e)

The training topics, methods and targeted groups within S & C.

The nature and content of training will inevitably need to be tailored to the needs of the relevant groups, for example:

- *Partners*: general overview of the system and its benefits possibly through executive training seminars.
- *Users*: instilling detailed user knowledge on how to operate the new system. Specific detailed applications training (including procedures, commands and data entry requirements and so on).
- *Users' managers*: giving an understanding of the elements of the system for which they are responsible, including particular business issues and security and control features related to a particular system. Possibly general training in basic computer literacy and user skills.

The sort of training provision might include:

- Seminars and workshops and so on.
- User manuals, "help lines" and dedicated support teams.
- Online computer-based support.
- On-the-job training while staff actively use the new system.
- Quality circles and discussion forums for users to address problem areas.
- Short demonstrations and the use of DVD/Video media support.
- Updates as users become familiar with the system and require further knowledge and skills.

This can be provided

- in-house
- outsourced to specialists or
- some combination.

Requirement (f)

Aims of a post-implementation review:

- Post-implementation review should be carried out as soon as the system is fully operational, in order to assess the effectiveness of the system, adjustments that may be required and lessons that can be learnt for the future.
- This should take place possibly between one month and no longer than 1 year after changeover is completed.
- The findings and recommendations from the post-implementation review should be formally reported on.

The specific aims of the review will include:

- Whether the system satisfies user needs.
- How the actual costs and benefit of the system compare with what was anticipated.
- Making recommendations for improvement (if necessary).
- Determining the quality of systems of change and project management.
- Making recommendations that will help shape future management of implementation and change initiatives where necessary.

Section C questions

Question 1

K Company is experiencing rapid change. Increasing competition necessitates continual updating of its product offerings, its technology and its methods of working. Like other companies, today K Company has to be responsive to frequently changing customer requirements, the challenges posed by fast-moving competitors and many other threats from a changing world.

One of the ways in which K Company might seek to cope with the challenges of the rapidly changing environment is to become a "learning organisation".

Requirements

(a) Advise K Company what would be involved in building a learning organisation.

(16 marks)

The changing environment has implications for K Company's selection process and, given the limitations of interviews and selection tests that constitute the traditional methods of selection, the company has decided to make use of an Assessment Centre (AC) to improve its chances of obtaining people who fit the needs of the company.

(b) Describe the key features of an Assessment Centre and explain why it is considered to be more effective than traditional methods of selection.

(14 marks)
(Total = 30 marks)

Question 2

You work for a bank, which has indicated that it would like to find out more about the possibility of exploiting new information and communication technologies within the company's marketing mix. You have been asked to write a short report that outlines possibilities and explains in detail any benefits that could accrue both immediately and in the longer term.

(30 marks)

Question 3

The performance appraisal process is now well-established in large organisations.

Requirements

(a) Describe briefly the most common objectives of a performance appraisal system.

(8 marks)

(b) Explain why appraisal systems are often less effective in practice than they might be, and advise what management can do to try to ensure their effectiveness.

(22 marks)
(Total = 30 marks)

Question 4

The working practices of the Finance Department of the Smog retailing organisation are out of date. It operates as if developments in communications and information technology in management accounting techniques – the increasing concern with the environment – demands for better corporate governance and the impact of globalisation had never happened.

But things are changing. A new chief executive has just been appointed and she intends to see that the Finance Department, like the rest of the organisation, will operate as efficiently as any of Smog's competitors. She has already seen to it that the department is re-equipped with the latest technology, and a new management information system (MIS) has been installed. Unfortunately, a lack of training has meant that as yet, the organisation has been unable to benefit fully from the investment in either the new technology or the new MIS.

Requirements

(a) Explain briefly how each of the developments noted in the first paragraph of the scenario has influenced the practice of management accounting in progressive organisations.

(12 marks)

(b) Assume that you have been charged with the development of HR in the Finance Department of Smog. Describe the various kinds of training and development programmes that would be required in order to make full use of the investment in the Finance Department and equip the staff to cope with the challenges of the modern era.

(18 marks)
(Total = 30 marks)

Question 5

B3 is a family-run personnel agency. It offers a range of services to both individuals and corporate clients (mainly local medium-sized organisations). The son of the managing director (MD) is currently studying for a specialist university business degree. His course includes a "management consultancy" module where students are required to analyse an organisation and identify a range of development options for the business. The MD's son's investigations of B3 have led to a consultancy report being produced, extracts of which include:

"B3 should maximise the opportunities offered by information technology to a greater extent. In particular:

- *Opportunity 1.* B3 could develop its recent successful experiment in e-cruitment (the identification of employment opportunities through the world wide web and the emailing of clients). Currently details of vacancies are collected and matched to individual client's search criteria. When a match is identified clients are emailed and, if they are interested, interviews arranged. This service is not offered by any of B3's main competitors. There is a difficulty, however, in that many companies have barred access to personal emails at work and web access to recruitment sites such as B3's site from their offices. Market research suggests that significant opportunities for m-cruitment (jobs by mobile telephones) also exist. Making use of recent software developments, a text message containing a job title and some contact details could be sent out to individual clients instead of an e-mail, so providing a more convenient and speedy service.

- *Opportunity 2.* Virtually all CVs are currently received in electronic form and a policy decision should be made to develop a paperless operating environment through the development of databases: so upgrading existing office technology.

Analysis of profit indicates that executive searches, corporate 'headhunting' and vacancy identification for individuals (traditional and especially e-cruitment) are all profitable activities.

Involvement in selection processes with corporate clients is unprofitable and should be discontinued. Instead B3 should identify clear guidelines for corporate clients to follow once the short-listing of candidates has occurred".

Requirements

(a) Evaluate the opportunities for B3 identified in the consultancy report.

(18 marks)

(b) Produce guidelines for the selection process that should be adopted by an organisation presented with a short-list of candidates.

(12 marks)
(Total = 30 marks)

Question 6

Requirements

(a) Using prescriptive, planned change theory, as outlined by Lewin and others, describe how any major new organisational initiative can be successfully implemented.

(15 marks)

Zed Bank operates in a fiercely competitive market and has decided to implement a number of important initiatives, including:

- enhancing its current services to customers by providing them with on-line internet and telephone banking services; and
- reducing costs by closing many of its rural and smaller branches (outlets).

In an attempt to pacify the employee representatives (the Banking Trade Union) and to reduce expected protests by the communities affected by branch closure, a senior Bank spokesperson has announced that the changes will be "incremental" in nature.

In particular, she has stressed that:

- the change will be implemented over a lengthy time period;
- there will be no compulsory redundancies;
- banking staff ready to take on new roles and opportunities in the on-line operations will be retrained and offered generous relocation expenses.

For customers, the Bank has promised that automatic cash dispensing machines will be available in all the localities where branches (outlets) close. Customers will also be provided with the software needed for Internet banking and other assistance necessary to give them quick and easy access to banking services.

The leader of the Banking Trade Union is "appalled" at the initiatives announced. He has argued that the so-called "incremental" change is in fact the start of a "transformational" change that will have serious repercussions, not only for the Union's members but also for many of the Bank's customers.

(b) Distinguish incremental change from transformational change. Explain why the Bank spokesperson and the trade union leader disagree over their description of the change

(15 marks)

(Total = 30 marks)

Question 7

The country Mythland contains several areas of high unemployment, one such area is where CX Beers were produced until recently. CX was an old, family-owned brewery that supplied licensed outlets, including local restaurants, with its beer. CX represented one of the last local brewers of any size, despite retaining many working practices that evolved at least a century ago. Situated on a (now) underused dockside site, the company had, over the years, invested little in plant and machinery and someone jokingly once suggested that much of the brewing equipment should rightfully be in a museum! The company was forced to cease trading last month, despite having an enthusiastic, long-serving, highly skilled workforce and a national reputation for the beer "CX Winter Warmer" (thanks to winning several national awards). The workforce, many of whom have only ever worked for CX Beers are now facing up to the difficulty of finding alternative employment.

In a press statement the owners said that the brewery's closure was sad for the area, the local workforce and traditionally brewed beer in general. The owners blamed the situation on inefficient and expensive brewing methods, fierce competition from large rival brewers and limited geographical sales. They also mentioned a dependence on seasonal sales that made cash flow difficult (35% over the Christmas period). They concluded that they would like the CX tradition to continue by selling the company as a going concern, however unlikely this was.

It is speculated that property developers may be interested in the site as the dockland area is showing signs of regeneration as a leisure and tourism attraction (thanks to the efforts of the Mythland government). However, two of CX's managers would like to save the business and are drawing up a business plan for a management buy-out. They have three main initiatives that they feel could, in combination, save the enterprise:

- Use the site as a basis for a "living" museum of traditionally brewed beer (with out of date brewing equipment and methods of working as an attraction);
- Produce bottled beer for sales in supermarkets;
- Employ a more flexible but suitably experienced workforce.

One of the managers (your former boss) has asked for your help in advising him how to draft a detailed human resource (HR) plan to inform the business plan.

Requirements

(a) Describe the main issues and stages involved in developing a human resource (HR) plan for the CX buy-out idea.

(18 marks)

(b) Discuss how the buy-out team can achieve workforce flexibility.

(12 marks)
(Total = 30 marks)

Question 8

NS Ltd is a regional chain of sports shops. The company was started in 1995 by Bruce Cohen, an ex-professional sportsman who played at international level. During his time as a sports professional Bruce became a good friend with the marketing representative of a large sports clothing wholesaler and distributor. When Bruce opened his sports clothing and equipment business he used his friend's company to supply the shop with all of its stock.

NS established itself quickly in the region, mainly due to Bruce's reputation locally. Successful trading has led to the present chain of five shops spread throughout the region. A significant element of NS's successful growth was the strong partnership that had developed between NS and its sole supplier.

However, in the last 2 years trading conditions have become increasingly tough. The continued expansion of large National sports shop chains into the area has meant increased choice and lower prices for consumers. In addition, Bruce's friend has moved on to a new company and his replacement seems more concerned with ensuring that the National chains are satisfied rather than NS.

The Financial Director believes that the company's downturn has been due, in large part, to the way in which NS has purchased their stock. She has recommended to the Board that NS should take a more strategic view of purchasing. The Sales Director strongly disagrees. His view is that the role of purchasing is to order the goods they are asked to order. He believes that the success of the company is solely dependant on identifying what products customers want and pricing them competitively.

Requirements

You are the Management Accountant at NS and have just attended a conference entitled "Supply Chain Management for Success". Bruce, in his capacity as Managing Director, has asked you to address the Board on the role purchasing could play in the future of NS Ltd.

(a) Describe the four stages of Reck and Long's "Strategic Positioning Tool" and identify the present position of NS Ltd, according to the Sales Director, and the supply management approach, as advocated by the Financial Director.

(10 marks)

(b) Advise the Sales Director of how effective supply chain management can contribute to the operational performance of NS Ltd.

(10 marks)

(c) If NS is to take a more strategic approach to purchasing, outline the five elements, identified by Cousins, that the Board must concentrate on to ensure a cohesive approach.

(10 marks)
(Total = 30 marks)

Question 9

B & G is a large manufacturing firm that is well known as a "good employer". Over the past few years, B & G has experienced difficult times with reducing sales and mounting losses. In desperation it employed management consultants to analyse its situation. The consultants have concluded that the downturn in sales is permanent and that B & G needs to reduce its workforce by 50% over the next year in order to survive. Reluctantly, B & G's board of directors has accepted these findings, including the need to reduce the number of staff. The directors have also agreed to act as honestly and as fairly as possible, but realise that any changes they propose will be unpopular and may meet with resistance.

Requirements

(a) Discuss what initiatives B & G can take to achieve the job reductions needed given the company's reputation for being a good employer. (Your answer should include reference to appropriate support for any individuals affected.)

(15 marks)

(b) Discuss the potential strategies available in order to overcome resistance to change, and identify those strategies that would be most suitable for B & G.

(15 marks)
(Total = 30 marks)

Question 10

NS is a large insurance company. The company is structured into four Divisions and supported by a small headquarters that includes the personnel function (recently renamed the Human Resources (HR) Division). The post of Head of HR is vacant following the retirement of the long serving post holder, and the HR strategy is in urgent need of review and revision.

NS has recently announced a new corporate initiative of continuous improvement through the empowerment of its workforce. The Chief Executive explained: "we value our people as our most prized asset. We will encourage them to think, challenge and innovate. Only through empowering them in this way can we achieve continuous improvement. Staff will no longer be expected just to obey orders, from now on they will make and implement decisions to bring about continuous improvement. We want to develop clear performance objectives and be more customer focused."

Your line manager is one of the four Divisional directors and will soon form part of a panel that will interview candidates for the vacant role of HR director. She is particularly keen to ensure that the successful candidate would be able to shape the HR Division to the needs of the organisation. She is aware of your CIMA studies and has asked for your help in preparing for the interview.

Requirements

Produce outline notes for your Divisional director which discuss the main points you would expect candidates to highlight in response to the following two areas she intends to explore with candidates at the interview, specifically:

(a) The likely role that the HR Division will perform in the light of the changing nature of the organisation; and

(15 marks)

(b) The aspects of the HR strategy that will change significantly, given the nature of recent developments within NS.

(15 marks)
(Total = 30 marks)

Question 11

SX is a growing company that has successfully used local radio advertising for the past few years to raise awareness of its products. It supplies fresh "quality" sandwiches, home baked snacks, the finest coffee and freshly squeezed fruit juices for sale at premium prices in petrol filling stations. Products are produced by traditional methods from very early morning by a team of employees at a central depot and are delivered throughout the day by a few casual workers in a fleet of vehicles.

SX has for the first time undertaken a full strategic marketing planning process. One weakness identified was that the number of deliveries required was increasing, while some of the drivers were becoming increasingly unreliable. The owner is worried that this may create an unfavourable image with customers and lead to delays in delivery.

In terms of opportunities, the owner of SX is now aware that by using technology to a greater degree and identifying customer needs more fully, the firm can grow at an even greater rate. To this end it is proposed that time saving food preparation and packaging equipment be purchased. This will mean considerably fewer people involved in food preparation but the owner feels that some employees could be redeployed as drivers on a permanent basis. The role of driver would be redefined, and in addition to making deliveries, he or she would be expected to:

- get direct feedback from customers;
- persuade petrol stations to take new product lines;
- provide intelligence on competitor's products and likely future demand;
- hopefully persuade other petrol stations and outlets (such as railway stations and newspaper shops) to stock SX products.

The owner is keen to progress change, consequently:

- The Head of delivery and customer relationships has been tasked with developing new job and person details for the driver posts. These will then be discussed with existing food preparation staff.
- A marketing action plan will soon be prepared based on the strategic marketing plan, which will contain immediate marketing issues and actions required. Some detail is already available on people and price so the main areas to consider are product, place and promotion.

Requirements

(a) Based on your understanding of the changes proposed by SX, identify the main issues that will be included in the marketing action plan and discuss the implications of these. Your response should consider issues of product, place and promotion only.

(15 marks)

(b) Based upon the information given to you concerning SX, and your own study and experience, produce a draft job description for the redefined post of driver.

(15 marks)
(Total = 30 marks)

Question 12

The B Company, a long-established food company with about 200 employees, is experiencing a number of problems including the need to implement new hygiene regulations, changes in consumer tastes, rising costs of materials, increasing competition and a demand for higher pay from its employees. But, rather than rising to the challenges as was the case in the past, the current staff seem unable to respond effectively. Morale is generally at a low level, departments are not co-operating and there have even been instances of conflict between quality control and operations. There also seems to be a lack of confidence in the management in general and a feeling that the company has lost direction.

A consultant called in to assist the B Company has recommended the use of techniques drawn from the field of organisational development as one means of tackling B's problems.

Requirements

(a) Describe the overall approach of organisational development. Illustrate your answer with examples of how particular organisations have applied this approach.

(14 marks)

(b) Using your knowledge of organisational development, explain how you would use the methods/techniques of organisational development to deal with the problems in the B Company.

(16 marks)
(Total = 30 marks)

Question 13

The Store Manager of the D Company, a pottery retailer, is primarily concerned with ensuring that she has sufficient employees with the right training to keep the store operating efficiently. The HR Manager accepts the need for training, but is also concerned to enhance the competitive advantage of the D Company by encouraging employee development. The ultimate aim of the HR Manager is to help the D Company to become "a learning organisation".

Requirements

(a) Describe how the Store Manager's idea of "training" differs from the HR Manager's notion of "employee development".

(10 marks)

(b) Discuss the key features of a "learning organisation". Explain how the HR Manager could assist the D Company to become a learning organisation.

(20 marks)
(Total = 30 marks)

Question 14

S Company develops accountancy software for small to medium-sized businesses. S Company was established 15 years ago by a graduate in accounting. Despite an increasingly competitive environment, it has grown and diversified to become a global provider of specialised accountancy software.

In order to cope with the increasing size and diversity of the business, additional levels of management and control systems have been introduced, including additional policies, rules and procedures. Unfortunately, the increase in bureaucracy is having the effect of slowing down the decision-making processes and limiting ideas for new software development.

The CEO is aware of the conflict between the structural changes and the need for continuous creativity and innovation that are critical to new software development and the future success of the business, but is not sure how to overcome the problem.

Requirements

(a) Explain
  (i) why formal control systems are increasingly necessary as an organisation grows and diversifies; and
  (ii) why the use of bureaucratic forms of control in S Company might limit creativity and innovation.

(16 marks)

(b) Discuss how S Company could balance control with autonomy to assist continuous creativity and innovation.

(14 marks)
(Total = 30 marks)

Question 15

Following a benchmarking exercise, A, the CEO of B Company, a food manufacturer, decided that several changes were required in order to maintain competitiveness. These included:

- a change in structure in order to improve the focus of expertise on particular products and customers;
- tighter control of costs; and
- the introduction of a more entrepreneurial culture.

Having decided that these changes were necessary, A emailed all heads of the departments indicating that during the following few months, the company would move from a functional structure to a divisional structure. Existing functional heads would be interviewed for senior posts in the newly created divisions in open competition with other applicants. The job specification for the new divisional heads included a requirement that the new heads would drive the changes, including a rapid transition to a more entrepreneurial culture and the implementation of new control mechanisms to contain costs. He put the change programme in the hands of the head of HR and went off on a 2-week overseas business trip asking that he be kept informed of progress.

When the CEO returned from his business trip, he found that no progress had been made towards the changes he had requested. The head of HR informed him that heads of departments were reluctant to discuss the intended changes and that some had even talked about resignation from the company.

Requirements

(a) Describe the key mistakes made by the CEO in the way he went about introducing the proposed changes in B Company.

(15 marks)

(b) Given the situation on the CEO's return, advise him on what he should do in order to ensure that the changes could be successfully implemented.

(15 marks)
(Total = 30 marks)

Question 16

Banking services within the country of Everland are provided exclusively by a few well established banks, all offering broadly similar "traditional" banking services. Overall, the industry performance is viewed from within as satisfactory and historically all banks have maintained stable profits and employment levels. Marketeers would describe the industry as being classically "product oriented". The profile of senior Everland bank officials and managers is of well-qualified professionals, possessing long banking industry experience and considerable financial skills. Within the combined workforce other business skills (in, for instance, HR or marketing) are noticeably lacking.

In the external environment, the government will soon pass new legislation that will effectively break the oligopoly-type position of banks and open the market up to other providers. Senior bank officials, however, are unconcerned, feeling that banks are in "reasonable shape" to face any new challenge.

You work for the Everland Banking Advisory Group (EBAG), an independent body, and have been asked to analyse the banking industry in the country of Utopia to identify lessons that might be learnt. Your investigation reveals that since the sector opened up to more competition, a much wider range of financial institutions offer banking services. Despite this, banks in Utopia have all prospered over the past few years. This is thanks to wide-ranging changes in how they operate, the products and services they offer and their organisational structures. You identify some significant trends within the banking industry of Utopia, including:

- The use of marketing techniques.
- A clearer focus on customers (who have become increasingly more demanding).
- A new generation of bank employees, many with commercial backgrounds.
- Banks now exhibiting a strong sense of ethical and social responsibilities towards customers.

Requirements

(a) Discuss the dangers to Everland banks if they do not change.

(12 marks)

(b) Discuss the types of change that Everland banks could be making in order to survive and prosper.

(18 marks)
(Total = 30 marks)

Question 17

CQ4 is a leading European industrial gas production company. CQ4's directors are each responsible for a geographical region containing several small strategic business units (SBUs). SBU managers report in monthly review meetings in great detail to their directors. CQ4 is showing signs of declining profitability and a new chief executive has been appointed and wishes to address the situation. She has complete freedom to identify organisational problems, solutions and strategies.

At their annual conference she tells SBU managers that they hold the key to improved company performance. She has a vision of CQ4 achieving longer-term strategic goals of increases in profitability, risk taking and innovation. Under the slogan "support not report" directors will in future support and provide assistance to their managers to a greater degree, and the frequency and detail of reporting by managers will be reduced.

She announces two new initiatives "to address the lost years when managers were prevented from delivering truly excellent CQ4 performance":

- Revision of the existing performance appraisal system. Bonuses paid on turnover will be replaced by performance related pay for achievement of individual "performance target contracts". Individual SBU managers will sign contracts to deliver these targets. Performance will now be reviewed at yearly rather than monthly meetings with directors. The remuneration and reward package will be adjusted appropriately with the current emphasis on increasing turnover shifting to profitability and innovation.
- A structural review to focus resources and efforts of SBUs on improving net profit. Part of the restructuring will involve SBUs no longer providing their own "enabling" services such as finance, information technology, and health and safety. These "distractions from doing the real job" will in future be organised centrally. SBUs will be given far greater responsibility, autonomy and influence over their own profitability.

She tells managers that she is stripping away the things that stop them doing their job properly. In return they must manage their SBU in the way they see most appropriate. They will be better rewarded and "star achievers" will be fast tracked to senior positions. SBU managers are informed that the HR department has already been tasked with redesigning the remuneration and reward package.

Informal discussions amongst managers afterwards confirm that the new chief executive's message has been well received. Comments such as "work might be more enjoyable without central interference" and "for the first time I can do my job properly" were overheard.

Requirements

(a) Explain the thinking behind the two initiatives announced by the new chief executive using Herzberg's motivation-hygiene (dual factor) theory as a framework.

(15 marks)

(b) Discuss the factors that should be taken into account by the HR department when redesigning the remuneration and reward package for SBU managers.

(15 marks)
(Total = 30 marks)

✓ Section C answers

Answer 1

(a) The notion of the learning organisation has been discussed by a number of writers including Senge, Argyris, Schon and Pedlar. According to the most famous advocate of organisational learning, Peter Senge, there are five core competences that K Company will need to develop to become a learning organisation. These are:

- the building of a shared vision;
- personal mastery;
- utilisation of mental models;
- team learning; and
- systems thinking.

Building a shared vision is necessary to ensure people are focused around a common sense of purpose. If there is no shared vision about the organisation, its purpose and values; then learning only occurs when there is a crisis that brings everyone temporarily together. Personal mastery of learning emphasises the need for continuous learning and self-development.

It is worth adding here, however, that for K Company to become a learning organisation, more than personal mastery is required. As Pedlar has emphasised, a learning organisation is different from simply the summation of the learning of individuals in an organisation. Though organisations do not have brains, they have cognitive systems and memories that preserve certain behaviours, mental maps, norms and values over time. Individuals may come and go, but if their learning has been passed on to others in the organisation, the benefit of their learning to the organisation continues. Working with mental models is one way for people to recognise their unconscious assumptions, and to appreciate how alternative actions at work could create a different reality.

A learning organisation requires individuals to come together and act as teams. Therefore, personal mastery of learning has to be accompanied by team learning so that it can be practised when groups of people have to confront controversial issues and make difficult decisions. Such team learning skills do not come naturally, and this probably explains the poor results of team working in some companies.

Systems thinking emphasises the importance of understanding interrelationships, rather than breaking problems down into discrete parts. It is a matter of coming to see how the various parts of the organisation fit together to form a whole functioning entity and how changes in one part of the organisation impact on other parts.

Senge also suggests that companies like K Company might find it useful to shift to a learning organisation in a series of stages. The first stage might be primarily concerned with frontline workers, and management's task is to:

- champion continual improvement;
- remove bureaucratic barriers to improvement; and
- support initiatives such as benchmarking and quality training that drive process improvements.

The second stage might be concerned with encouraging new ways of thinking about how organisational processes (for example sales order entry, manufacturing and customer satisfaction) interact. During this stage, the primary focus of change is on the managers themselves.

The third stage is one in which learning becomes institutionalised as an inescapable way of life for managers and workers.

Other writers like Pedlar have emphasised that the learning organisation should be regarded as a process rather than a product. So for K Company the emphasis should be on continuous learning rather than a particular end-state of knowledge because rapid change demands new ways of doing things, and new skills and knowledge to enable the organisation to compete.

Finally, Pedlar notes that the learning organisation does not come in turnkey form. In other words, it is not simply a matter of installing it like a piece of equipment, but is a continuous process of learning that involves everyone in the organisation on an ongoing basis. K Company will need to be aware of this. Such a change will require a great deal of commitment and effort and it may be that K Company will require a cultural change.

(b) An Assessment Centre (AC) is defined as "the assessment of a group of individuals by a team of assessors using a comprehensive and interrelated set of techniques". An AC does not necessarily mean a physical centre, but is a particular approach and philosophy. It is important to ensure that jobs have been analysed and the results classified to provide a list of criteria or competences around which the AC's should be designed.

Assessment techniques such as role-play, simulations, "in-tray" exercises, negotiations, presentations and tests are designed to ensure that there is a sufficient number of the right kind of assessment tools to measure all the relevant dimensions.

The superiority of the AC approach over traditional methods lies in the range of methods employed to assess candidates and the duration of the period of testing. AC testing often takes a number of days, whereas conventional interviews often last less than an hour. The AC approach also enables the assessors to observe the actual behaviour and performance of candidates in a whole range of situations, whereas interviewing, which is the most common method of selection, only allows observation in a single, highly artificial situation.

The available research to date suggests that ACs have a higher validity in terms of predicting future performance than the more commonly used methods of references, application forms and interviews.

Beaumont (1993) reports on research shows that "the probability of selecting an 'above average performer' on a random basis was 15%, a figure that rose to 35% using appraisal and interview data and to 76% using assessment centre results". Thus, ACs have been shown to have good, predictive validity and this is significantly improved when more selection devices are used.

It should be noted, however, that while more effective, ACs are more expensive to set up and administer and this is one reason why smaller companies, in particular, do not make use of them.

Answer 2

To: Marketing Director
From: Accountant
Date: xx/xx/xx

Subject: Exploitation of new information and communication technologies
The following report has been prepared in response to the above remit, using a bank as the main focus for the ICTs. There are several ICTs and it is proposed to consider each one in turn. The target audience is technophiles and aspiring technophiles, who between them make up approximately 50% of consumers.

Internet
A website could be developed for the bank that would include details of the full product range of the bank. The range might include mortgages, insurance, current and deposit accounts, currency exchange, cards. It could be updated with new products. Any person logging on to the site could be entered on the database and contacted later. The design of the site should be particularly focused on the above-mentioned groups. School and university students should be a particular focus group since the Government is committed to increase the number of computers in education and their ICTs. The reason being that once a customer has chosen a bank they tend to stay with the same one.

Videoconferencing
This is another ICT that could be used once the above reports had been circulated for a management meeting. The meeting could take place using videoconferencing. It would also enable more flexible working patterns. Time wasted in travelling to meetings, travelling abroad, would be minimalised by this technology. This could also be developed into virtual banking, as in virtual reality games. The customer does not need to physically enter a bank to obtain details of the services provided, or use the service. It could be carried out using virtual banking. A combination of menu choices, supported by videoconferencing, would enable any customer linked up to the system to carry out any banking task without moving from their computer.

Smart cards (electronic purse)
These cards allow purchase of items up to a predetermined limit – a value of credits. They are another step towards the cashless society. Some banks are already using them to pay for meals and refreshments within the bank. The cards would be of benefit to the bank's customers as they would be supplying a service for paying for many purchases, such as shopping, parking, drinks, books, meals and so on. Many banks are supplying smart cards to university students to enhance the service to them.

The benefits for banks from smart cards come from the replacement of cash and cheque transactions, and in the ability to put multiple applications on the same card. This would enable the cash dispensing service to be reduced, thus freeing staff to deal with specific customer enquiries.

CD-ROM
These can be used to store significant amounts of data, both text and multimedia. Sound, pictures and text can be transmitted using modems, phone lines and satellite links. This means that they could be used for marketing the services of the bank, for training the staff and so on.

Database marketing
With new software available, the possibilities of holding extensive information on the bank's customers and using it intelligently are limitless. As a bank, detailed information on customers is already being stored; details such as address; earnings; where they purchase goods and services; when they pay them; how they pay their debts; their buying preferences. By using appropriate software, the market could be segmented more accurately, customers targeted specifically and products positioned accordingly. Gaps in the market could be identified and filled. Retaining existing customers and extending the range of products sold to customers is the most profitable means of developing new business.

Home banking
Many banks are already offering with home banking. The service can be effected through a modem, phone and video-conferencing links, depending on the provider, but experience has demonstrated that broadband connectivity is required. Currently, home banking provides most of the services of the bank without the use of letters or the usual communication forms. Cheques can be issued; standing orders and direct debits set up; balance enquiries. This service allows more sophisticated targeting of the market and facilitates the opportunity to promote additional services (mortgages etc.) to the customer. Partly as a result of this the number of high street banks is declining, thus the savings are significant. The savings in paper, both for the bank and the customer are also worthwhile. Home banking also enables the bank to add value to the service provided to customers, by promoting other services which the customer has not yet requested.

Voice recognition computers
Security within the banking sector is a continual problem. The use of signatures and photographs to ensure security of the customer's and bank's information is of very low technology. The use of finger prints and possibly voice recognition would enhance the security of many bank transactions and be another value-added product for the bank to sell on.

Mobile phones
A recent report on ICTs in the office environment highlighted the fact that mobile phones were equated with email, local and wide area networks, and were seen as critical factors to the success of the surveyed companies. The advanced features now becoming available on mobile phones suggest that this is another ICT that the banking sector should not ignore. Displays are being incorporated into the mobile phone, which could be used by both bank staff and customers alike to exchange information.

EPOS, EFPTOS and EDI
These are also ICTs. Organisations such as retail stores and manufacturers have reaped significant benefits through EPOS, by being provided with more information about stock control and consumer behaviour. EFTPOS has facilitated the delivery of customer service and allows more flexible payment methods. EDI links with suppliers allow just-in-time stock replenishment and improved production planning by suppliers to take place through a phone line, ISDN or other communication medium.

Conclusion
There are significant benefits in using ICTs to the banking and other industries. Some of the benefits will be immediate and can be secured in the short term with minimal cost. Database management, modems, the Internet and mobile phones fall into this category.

Other benefits are long term, requiring considerable discussion in deciding whether to implement them or not. This is because they are very expensive and time-consuming to install and may soon become out of date and out of fashion. Home banking, videoconferencing and smart cards falls into this category.

Answer 3

(a) The objectives of a formal performance appraisal system usually include the following:

- The assessment of an individual's current level of job performance. This is useful as a base line against which performance can be measured in future. It is also useful as a means of deciding how the individual has improved since the last performance appraisal.
- The determination of potential performance. This is particularly important if the individual is being considered for promotion in the organisation. It is useful to have on record the potential of staff in readiness for when vacancies occur.
- The identification of the employees' current strengths and weaknesses can be considered as a more detailed consideration of the first objective about the current level of job performance, but the identification of weaknesses helps in deciding training needs, while identification of strengths is useful if management needs to call upon these in other parts of the organisation.
- The identification of training and development needs can be seen to follow an evaluation of strengths and weaknesses, but the identification of training needs may arise for reasons other than the capabilities of individual employees. They may arise from any number of sources such as new demands made by changing legislation, new technology and so on.
- Assisting the motivation of individuals by providing feedback on performance. The formal performance appraisal interview represents an opportunity to provide positive feedback to employees on their performance and to set new targets and challenges for the coming period along with a reminder of possible rewards.
- As a means of collecting information for succession planning. This has already been noted, but it reminds us of the need for systematic consideration of the HR plan for the forthcoming time period and of the need to collect information on all personnel about their suitability for promotion or perhaps even for early retirement.

(b) The ineffectiveness of a formal performance appraisal system has its roots in the frailty of human judgement, inappropriate design and in poor implementation of the systems. Because assessments of this kind involve human judgement by some individuals of the performance of other individuals, problems of subjectivity necessarily arise. The lack of objective criteria in aspects of performance that are difficult to quantify leaves room for doubt on the part of the person appraised that they have been fairly judged and to possible disputes about any rewards that might be based on such judgements.

Performance appraisal systems are also often less effective than they might otherwise be because of inappropriate design. Some performance appraisal systems are ineffective because:

- they focus on aspects of the person rather than on the performance of the task;
- they are designed in such a way as to encourage the appraiser to opt for a middle category of performance rather than to consider the whole range of performance measures.

In addition, performance appraisal systems are often less effective than they might otherwise be because of poor implementation. Such poor implementation is based in turn on a variety of causes including the following:

- First, the lack of time and resources in many organisations for effective implementation. Performance appraisal is normally carried out by line managers who have many other pressing duties in addition to that of the formal appraisal of their staff. In many organisations the annual appraisal comes to be regarded as a necessary bind that interrupts the essential work of production.
- Associated with the lack of time and resources is lack of appropriate training. This may include not only lack of training in the actual process of conducting appraisal interviews in an appropriate manner, but also a lack of attitudinal training. The effect of this inadequate training is that many managers do not have the skills or the motivation to conduct the appraisal process in an effective manner. In fact, it is a common claim among managers that they appraise their subordinates on an ongoing informal manner throughout the year and so do not see the need for systematic formal performance appraisal systems.

In progressive organisations, these problems associated with performance appraisal have been recognised and steps taken to limit their detrimental effect.

As far as the problem of subjectivity is concerned, Human Resource Management departments have moved away from trait personality scales that seek to measure the personal qualities of individuals. This is because these are seen as more prone to subjective judgement than measurements of outcomes and behaviourally anchored observation scales (use of list of key job items against which are ranged a number of descriptors or just the use of two extreme statements of anticipated behaviour). The concentration on job outcomes or results is thus recommended rather than the focus on the person, as was often the case in early appraisal systems.

In recent years, the use of competency-based frameworks has been introduced. These focus on the performance of the person rather than on the qualities of the person but the whole issue of competence measurement itself is still the subject of considerable debate.

The problem of poor implementation depends upon the attitude of senior management. Only if management take performance appraisal seriously and commit the necessary resources for training and the time for the conduct of formal appraisal interviews can the appraisal system work effectively.

This commitment of senior management must also extend to providing resources for the follow-up to the appraisal interviews. In particular, a serious attempt to address training and development needs, identified during the interviews, must be made or those appraised are likely to lose faith in the whole process. In fact, the same point can be made about anything agreed between those conducting the appraisal and the individuals being appraised. Unless the jointly agreed decisions are followed up with action, the whole exercise comes to be seen as a form filling exercise that has to be endured on a periodic basis.

Answer 4

(a) The role of the management accountant is changing because of changes in the business environment, associated changes in organisations and the development of new management accounting techniques.

According to a number of recent surveys, the key drivers of change in management accounting include communications and information technology, organisational restructuring, globalisation and internationalisation and quality and continuous improvement initiatives. Other changes include a trend towards the outsourcing of routine accounting transactions, the development of new management accounting techniques, developments in the education and training of accountants, and the spread of accounting knowledge amongst an increasing number of managers.

The major changes to *the practice* of the management accounting role arising from these pressures are as follows:

- First, there has been a reduction in the importance of the recording of transactions and "books of accounts" as a result of developments in IT. The development of accounting software packages allows easier collection, storage, manipulation and accessing of financial data. This data is also now more accessible to managers who are now much better educated both in accounting matters and in the use of IT than in the past. The developments in IT have also made location of the management accounting function less important than in the past. The use of electronic means of data transmission means that accounting transactions can be carried out at remote and cheaper locations than in major cities. Indeed, some large companies have taken advantage of these developments and outsourced their routine transactions to either in-house or third-party service centres. Increasingly much of the routine accounting work is being carried out by what are referred to as "pseudo accountants".
- Second, the importance of strategic financial planning has increased. The trend towards a more proactive strategic role in business decision-making is being driven by demands from chief executives for better advice in an increasingly turbulent and uncertain environment. The developments in the education and training of management accountants are providing the means to enable accountants to meet these demands.
- Third is the development of a number of new management accounting techniques such as ABC, benchmarking and the balanced scorecard. The advent of software packages that allow accountants to conduct "what if" analysis has also improved the armoury of management accountants to carry out their analytical tasks more efficiently and to present relevant and timely information to managers.
- Fourth, environmental matters and the demands of corporate governance are increasing the requirement on management accountants to provide new kinds of information for a wider range of stakeholders. Environmental pressure groups representing the public are concerned about the treatment of waste and the safety procedures and safety records of companies. The extent to which management accountants will have responsibility for these matters is open to debate, but they are part of the information needs of management.
- Fifth, the globalisation of business means that accountants employed in global companies become more and more involved in reporting matters that affect the corporation in other countries. Details of the basis of trading with foreign countries such as fluctuations in exchange rates, political payments at home and abroad, labour policies in the Third World and so on must be accounted for. So

also must the influence of bodies like the World Bank and the World Trade Organisation as well as other countries" policies on safety, health and green issues, pension schemes and other related issues.

(b) The training and development programmes required in the finance department of the Smog retailing organisation can usefully be divided into two kinds. First, those to enable the staff to make use of the investment in the new technology; and second, those designed to enable staff to cope effectively with the other changes that are affecting the work of personnel involved in Accounting and Finance.

Traditionally, it has been common to treat training and development as if they were separate processes with training usually conceived of as being concerned with vocational studies for non-managerial employees while "development" has been the term used to talk about the education of managerial staff.

Recent thinking in HRM, however, has thrown this distinction into question. In a philosophy in which all employees are considered as valuable assets to the company, it is argued that all staff should be developed as well as trained. The trend today, therefore, is to see training and development as linked processes in which training is seen as part of and a precondition for development.

As far as training to use the new technology and information systems concerned, two types of programme are probably necessary. The first type would include in-house programmes to train personnel in the use of the company's new management information system. Such programmes are usually best carried out on the actual system out of office hours. The advantage of such an in-house programme is that it avoids the transfer of training problems that off-the-job training often suffers from. These commonly occur because trainees do not get the opportunity to practise their newly acquired skills or to apply the principles they learned on the training course when they return to their place of work.

Depending on the complexity of the system involved, some off-the-job training might also be useful either before or after the in-house training, but this is something that can only be decided properly after a careful examination of the relative advantages and disadvantages of the two types of programme.

Training and development to cope with the other changes facing the staff in the Smog Finance department would probably be best conducted off-the-job over a longer time period. The development in management accounting techniques requires first that accountants become familiar with the techniques and then a period of practice to develop competence in their use. On-the-job training would only become relevant, once the department concerned had adopted the new techniques and it looks from the brief scenario as if staff would need some updating and familiarisation before such techniques could be introduced.

The demands for environmental reporting, responsiveness to the demands required by new models of corporate governance and the demands of a more global economy are probably best dealt with as part of a more general education programme conducted by specialists off-the-job with occasional training sessions in-house to discuss actual measures that the department needs to adopt to cope with these changes.

Answer 5

Requirement (a)

Evaluation of the opportunities for B3

Opportunity 1

The opportunities are those offered by information technology (IT), In the case of Opportunity 1 this relates to the potential offered by the advances in technology.

The proposal is that B3 could extend e-cruitment to m-cruitment. When e-cruitment was introduced it was apparently "recent", "experimental" and not offered by competitors. Evidently it was introduced alongside "traditional" services, presumably the use of older technologies such as post and telephone The proposal could be viewed as being worthy for a number of reasons:

Extended service offering
e-cruitment has proven to be both popular and profitable. The proposal involves extending this experiment using text messaging. To introduce m-cruitment **instead** of other methods would be unwise. Instead, a more sensible approach would be to offer clients an option of either:

- "traditional" services;
- e-cruitment; or
- m-cruitment

This would expand the company's expertise and range of service offering.

Positive image projection
Potential clients undoubtedly would view this as a positive attempt by the company to tailor its services to the individual's own needs and preferences.

Enhance competitive strategy
e-cruitment has involved B3 in successfully differentiating its service from other competitors. Competitors are likely to copy this approach soon. A differentiation strategy such as this suggests that B3 needs to stay one step ahead, hence m-cruitment could be seen as a natural and desirable development.

The problems with this proposal include:

IT, IS costs and expertise
As long as B3 has the expertise and technology available to provide the service there will be no difficulty. (The experiment with e-cruitment suggests that there is no cultural resistance to the use of new technology.) If, however, additional costs are involved in time, training and software, m-cruitrnent might be an expensive distraction.

Ethical implications
Many companies have barred access to personal emails at work and web access to recruitment sites such as B3's site from their offices, m-cruitment is portrayed as a means of overcoming this. Although B3 would be meeting its individual clients needs, it would be frustrating companies who do not want their employees to search out new jobs in works time. This could be viewed as unethical.

Damaged reputation amongst corporate clients
B3 has corporate clients, mainly local medium sized organisations. It could adversely affect future business opportunities if employers realise that B3 is acting unethically.

Image of the company
Text is impersonal and lacks human interaction (even more so than emails). This could project an image to potential customers of being distant, impersonal and uncaring.

On balance, it might seem sensible to trial m-cruitment for a period of time (say 6 months) and assess the outcomes.

Opportunity 2

The opportunities are those offered by information technology (IT). In the case of Opportunity 2, it is the potential to use IT to run information systems (IS). The proposal is that a paperless operating environment should be developed.

In support of the proposal:

Potential
At the moment there appears to be a high degree of technology uptake and B3 makes use of web-based technology including email. In addition, "virtually all" client CVs are in electronic form.

Image
A paperless environment could project a favourable image to potential clients. It could also be a springboard for the company to expand beyond its regional base.

However, it might sound modern and exciting but experience of other organisations has proved that it is an elusive concept in practice. There are several difficulties associated with this proposal, including:

Cost
The report suggests that it will involve upgrading existing office technology. The benefits of a paperless office would have to be persuasive to justify this and other costs.

Implications
The report suggests a need to "develop databases". This may in itself be insufficient to achieve a paperless office.

Resistance by clients
Some individuals and organisations are reticent to trade over the web. These clients may be "lost" to competitors using more traditional trading methods,

Security and backup
The development of secure sites especially for the transfer of personal details and payment transfers would need to be carefully planned and installed. As sensitive data such as CVs are to be stored, there needs to be high levels of security and practices such as disaster recovery planning and risk assessment to consider.

On balance, paperless trading might more sensibly be viewed as an ultimate goal that the company works towards rather than a short-term strategy involving replacement of all existing practices.

Requirement (b)

Guidelines for selection processes for adoption

(Following advertisement of vacancy, preliminary contact with potential candidates, initial screening and final shortlist of agreed candidates.)

Agreement of selection criteria and testing method

- Use of person specification and job description and so on to determine criteria.
- Develop scorecards based on agreed criteria.
- Agree common questions to be asked of all candidates.
- Agree range, nature and complexity of selection processes to be used to test against criteria. (Processes must be cost-effective, that is justified in terms of the benefits of selecting good applicants for the particular job in question.) Processes will include formal structured interviews (decide whether "one to one", tandem, panel, sequential and so on).

Testing against selection criteria
Review of formal application forms to determine areas of experience and so on that need to be explored through interview and so on.

Make arrangements for formal interviews and other candidate testing.

Administer formal interviews and candidate testing.

Processes should be:

- *Reliable*: give consistent results.
- *Valid*: accurately predict performance.
- *Fair*: candidates should be treated in a non-discriminatory way (for example in terms of race, gender, age and so on).

Choosing the most suitable candidate

- Final analysis and choice based on criteria.
- Approach successful candidate and make offer subject to reference and medical checks.
- Send official job "offer" letter on the same basis.
- Feedback to unsuccessful candidates,

Administration

- Conduct reference checks being mindful of accuracy of factual data presented by the candidate.
- Arrange for medical examination.
- Issue letter confirming terms and conditions of service including pay rate and start date.
- Tidy relevant paperwork and file to evidence the process.

Review
Conduct a critical review of the process including successful and unsuccessful aspects and lessons learnt. Disseminate this information and revise future practices accordingly.

Answer 6

Requirement (a)

In order to facilitate the implementation of a planned change such as that envisaged in the scenario, the following action steps have been found to be useful:

The first step in any change process is to diagnose the current situation to identify the source of problems (or opportunities for improvement). In a large organisation, this frequently leads to a rethinking of strategy, and a redefinition of the organisation's task or work.

Unfreeze
The second step is to identify or create dissatisfaction with the current state. As long as people are satisfied with the current state, they will not be motivated to change. Kurt Lewin, and later Warren Bennis, pointed out that people need to be "unfrozen" out of their inertia in order to be receptive to change.

But while creating dissatisfaction with the present state is important, it is also necessary to offer an attractive future state that organisational members will wish to achieve. A critical requirement for managing the transition state, therefore, is to develop and communicate a clear vision of the future.

It is, of course, essential to communicate the plan so that all stakeholders can see what the benefits are and what has be done to achieve these. Communication can be accomplished in a variety of ways, ranging from written communications to small group meetings, large briefing sessions, videotaped presentations and so on.

Movement
The third step is to build in participation in the change. Participation in the change can help to reduce resistance, build ownerships of the change, and thus motivate people to make the change work. Participation also facilitates the communication of information about what the change will be and why it has come about.

For a change to occur successfully, sufficient support needs to be put together to push through the change. Those groups that may oppose the change, such as some employees and some customers, have to be persuaded to change their minds. Other groups more positive to the change have to be included in the planning of the change so that their participation will motivate them. Still others, like the trade union may have to be dealt with by bargaining or negotiations. This represents the fourth step in the process.

Refreeze
A fifth step for managing the transition involves the use of a range of rewards to influence the behaviour of individuals, including the need to build in rewards for the behaviour that is desired, both during the transitional state and in the future state. The expectancy theory of motivation and behaviour in organisations suggests that people will tend to be motivated to behave in ways that they perceive as leading to desired outcomes. This implies that both formal and informal rewards must be identified and tied to the behaviour that is needed, both for the transition and for the future state. The most frequent problem is that organisations expect individuals to behave in certain ways while rewarding them for other conflicting behaviours.

Resources for the transition such as personnel, training expertise, consultative expertise, and so on must also be available to the management responsible for implementing change.

Sixth, in order to measure and control performance, the management's plan requires benchmarks, standards of performance and a specification of the responsibilities of key individuals and groups.

The final action step for implementation involves developing feedback mechanisms to provide managers with information on the effectiveness of the change and to provide data on areas that require additional attention or action. Devices such as surveys, focus groups, consultant interviews and so on, as well as informal communication channels, need to be developed and used during this period.

Once the change has been completed it is, of course, necessary to ensure that mechanisms are in place to maintain the new strategies, practices and processes – that is, in Lewin's terminology, to re-freeze the changes.

Requirement (b)

The term "incremental change" refers to relatively small changes. When these occur over an extended period of time such changes are sometimes referred to as "evolutionary". One way of defining incremental change within an organisation is to confine its use to those changes that can be accommodated without a change to the organisation's structure and culture.

In the case scenario, Zed Bank's spokeswoman is using the term "incremental change" in this sense. More particularly, she is arguing that the Bank is not doing anything radically new, except to use available Internet and telecommunications technology to improve customer service and to reduce the Bank's costs. The term "incremental change" implies that the change envisaged by the Bank can be easily accommodated within the Bank's existing organisation structure and culture and that such minor changes as will occur will be beneficial both for bank employees and customers. In arguing the case for the changes in this way, she is seeking to reassure the Bank's staff and customers that the changes will be to their advantage.

In order to distinguish bigger and more radical changes from the many small changes that affect organisations, the term, "transformational change" is often employed. In the organisational context, this is defined as a change that cannot be accommodated by the existing structure and culture of the organisation. Such changes require a major restructuring of the organisation and significant cultural changes.

Such transformational changes, it is argued, have widespread effects. The privatisation of the railways in the UK for instance might be considered one example in which the structure and culture of the organisations that make up the industry have undergone dramatic change. Similarly, one could cite the way in which new technology facilitated the transformation of particular organisations in the printing industry in the 1980's.

In the scenario, the trade union representative is using the term "transformational change", to argue that the changes being undertaken by Zed Bank are just the prelude to a revolutionary change in banking, which may mean the disappearance of retail banks from the high street and their replacement by Internet Banks. He hopes he can persuade bank employees that the nature of their work will change radically and that they will come to understand that some of them may ultimately face redundancy.

Similarly, he hopes, by using the term "transformational change", to bring to the notice of Zed Bank's customers, the possibility that the use of Internet Banking will result in the disappearance of branch banking – a form of banking which many of them value. His overall intention will be to reinforce support for his view that the changes proposed by Zed Bank are dramatic and will affect Bank employees and customers in a way that is disadvantageous to all.

Answer 7

Requirement (a)

Main issues and stages in developing a human resource plan.

Considerations

Human resource planning involves developing a plan for the acquisition, utilisation, improvement and retention of an organisation's human resources. Such a plan needs to be integrated into the broader process of business planning if it is to be useful. In this case CX managers' business plan for a management buy-out.

The HR plan will need to take account of and support the three main initiatives identified as part of the buy-out:

- Heritage "real ale" tours using the dated brewing equipment and methods of working as an attraction.
- Bottling beer for sales in supermarkets.
- Employing a more flexible but suitably experienced workforce.

The plan will need to reflect:

- How HR flexibility will be achieved.
- Retraining in new skills.
- Budgets, targets and standards.
- Reward systems.
- Responsibilities for implementation and control (including the appraisal process).
- Reporting procedures that will enable achievements to be monitored against the plan.

Consideration will need to be taken of what CX represents: tradition, national reputation and "real ale" production.

The plan itself will need to meet certain key criteria: it will need to be realistic, accurate, suitable, consistent and so on.

Stages

The HR planning process normally consists of four main phases:

- Conducting an audit of the existing human resources in the light of any corporate or business changes.
- Forecasting future demand for labour.
- Assessing the external labour market and forecasting supply.
- Establishing a plan reconciling demand and supply.

Applying this thinking to the scenario:

Auditing of the existing resources. Clearly there have been big changes and technically no existing human resources exist! However, as the shut down only happened last month and the workforce has specialist skills that are likely to be unused in an area of high unemployment, most will be available for reemployment. HR records can be accessed to determine key pieces of information. The selection process will be important to ensure that CX obtains people with the right skills and/or the potential to develop such skills.

Forecasting future demand for labour. Based on past experience a good estimate of minimum and maximum numbers required will be possible. In addition to numbers, the skill requirements of people are also important. Again, based on past experience, projections can be made. As there appear to be no proposals for new technology/automation re-equipping skills and numbers can be confidently predicted. However, a number of important factors need to be taken into account when forecasting demand:

- The introduction of a new product: bottled beer which will have new skill implications.
- The development of brewery tours which will have new skill implications.
- The seasonal nature of sales.
- Financial limits on manpower costs as part of the business plan (that is what can be afforded).

Assess the external labour market and forecasting supply. Supply is likely to be plentiful, due to unemployment and unique skills. It is possible to use personnel (HR) records as the database for analysis of the past CX workforce. From these records it is possible to derive a wide range of information about the numbers, current skill, age, training undertaken, performance levels and so on. This information can provide knowledge of the supply of labour available locally.

Establish a plan reconciling demand and supply. Having made an estimate of the labour required to staff the organisation and considered the supply of labour available, the next step is to put together action plans for the recruitment and, where necessary, retraining in new skills of the workforce so that the demand and supply of labour can be reconciled. Considerations of motivation are normally relevant as part of this stage. As the workforce was previously highly motivated, the opportunity to be part of a re-launch of CX that offers them employment means that this is less of a consideration.

It must be acknowledged that in reality the process is rarely as linear and sequential as these phases suggest and many aspects progress together.

Requirement (b)

Flexibility into the workforce.

Work at present is very seasonal (the winter months being heaviest) and although brewery tours and bottled beers may help smooth fluctuations in work, more flexibility in the workforce is demanded for the new company to survive. Change in practices is clearly required and the new CX organisation may take on a different form to the old one.

To provide for flexibility other companies have adopted various approaches: New forms of employment terms (for example fixed term contracts, part time contracts or systems of "annual hours") to smooth the use of staff over critical periods such as seasonal shortages. The annual hours approach could work well at CX brewery. Outsourcing certain functions to outside contractors rather than addressing directly. For CX this might mean all administrative, payroll and marketing functions for instance.

Handy's "shamrock" organisation with an employed core of professional workers, a contractual fringe providing specialist and non essential services and flexible part time and temporary workers might be one model for CX. (This is consistent with Atkinson's (1984) ideas for core employees and periphery workers on temporary or part-time contracts to buffer against changes in demand.)

For CX, flexibility may take one or several of a number of forms:

Numerical flexibility. The development of a numerically flexible workforce involves flexing the labour employed. Temporary, part time, short term contract working and sub-contracting are used in addition to full time employment. This might be achieved by only bringing in employees when they are needed (during the seasonal rush in the run up to Christmas). This is often referred to as a flexible firm approach.

Task or Functional flexibility. This involves recruiting and developing staff with a wide range of skills so that such an employee can carry out a range of tasks. This saves the company from having to employ as many specialist workers as it might otherwise have to and also means those employees can cover for each other in case of absence. A CX employee of the future might for instance be required to brew on one day, carry out vital maintenance on another, and conduct a brewery tour on the third.

Financial flexibility. This is often achieved through some form of performance related payment. This might be related to bottles produced, sales figures, numbers on brewery tours, achieving financial targets identified in the business plan and so on.

Answer 8

(a) Reck and Long's "Strategic Positioning Tool" positions the purchasing stage an organisation has reached on a continuum. There are four stages as follows:

Passive
In this stage purchasing acts upon the requests from other departments. Some departments may get involved in the detail. The purchasing function, therefore, places a purchase order based upon the product requirements, price, supplier and delivery requirements identified by the other department. Ultimately, this is a transaction processing role.

The views of the Sales Director are consistent with the Passive stage as he states that the role of purchasing is to order what they are asked to order. He sees the role of purchasing as secondary to other departments in contributing to the success of the organisation.

The fact that NS only uses a single supplier also suggests that the purchasing department is not proactive in finding the best supplier for products, prices or delivery. This is consistent with the passive stage.

Independent
This is a more professional approach to purchasing. This includes enhanced use of IT and greater communication between the purchasing team and other departments and suppliers.

At this stage the NS purchasing department would recognise the financial importance of their role. This would lead them to searching for best prices and suppliers in response to purchasing requests from the rest of the company.

Supportive
At the supportive stage the role of purchasing is recognised as essential to the success of the business. It is understood that purchasing has the potential to affect organisational performance in pursuit of its goals. It is likely that someone quite senior in the business becomes responsible for the purchasing function.

The purchasing department takes a proactive role in providing timely and accurate information to the rest of the business on prices and availability. There may now be certain items that the purchasing team recognise as important to the business and order independently.

The supportive stage is also likely to involve constant review of supplier's performance against predetermined performance measures.

Integrative

Purchasing is now seen as integral to competitive strategies. It is now part of the strategy itself rather than an implementation issue. As such, purchasing management should become involved in strategy planning and development of the business.

This is consistent with the views of the Financial Director at NS with her view that NS should take a more strategic view of purchasing.

Suppliers now become vital business partners. It is likely that in the past this may have been the case with the single supplier of NS. However, it seems more recently that their supplier is focusing on the larger players in the market. By taking an integrative approach NS can start to plan the future supply strategy to the business by looking at the number of suppliers it should use and developing long-term strategic partnerships. This should prevent the present situation re-occurring in the future.

(b) Slack and Lewis identify five core objective areas for operations: quality, speed, dependability, flexibility and cost. As purchasing is a key part of operations, these five areas can be used to identify how effective supply chain management, using an integrative approach as outlined in part a, can contribute to organisational performance.

Quality

By developing strategic partnerships in the value system, NS can work with their suppliers on ensuring the quality of goods supplied. In a retail environment, quality of supplies is essential as the goods are likely to go straight on to the shop floor without any further processing. By having assured quality from their suppliers, NS will save the cost of performing quality checks.

Any inferior quality goods are likely to be spotted by the customers of NS. This reflects badly on NS and can damage their reputation in the market place.

Quality issues can also cause conflict with suppliers. By assuring quality in their supplies NS can avoid the time, money and energy that would be spent on disputes with suppliers. The absence of conflict also aids a stronger supplier relationship.

Speed

Within the world of sports clothing and equipment fashions, tastes and technological developments change quickly. To be successful it is essential to keep up with this pace of change and aim to be first to market with the latest goods.

Through effective supply chain management, NS can ensure that they have the right suppliers to enable them to get to the market quickly with the most up-to-date goods. This can give them a competitive advantage.

In a fast moving, dynamic market, it is also important to have the shortest lead times possible with suppliers as a long lead time could mean goods arriving after the customer needs have changed. This could lead to obsolete stock that has to be sold off at reduced prices.

Speed of supply can also be important if a customer needs something unusual or specialist equipment. These items may need to be custom ordered. Speed of supply on such orders could determine the customer's choice of retailer.

Dependability

In a retail environment it is essential that NS has the right goods in store at the right time. If the right goods are not on the shelves then customers cannot purchase them. In the current situation, it seems unlikely that their present supplier would be completely dependable as they are more concerned with fulfilling the orders of the large National chains than those of NS.

As part of effective supply chain management, NS can reduce the problem of potential "stock-outs" by developing supply relationships with the most dependable suppliers. By developing long-term relationships with suppliers, and so ensuring the supplier future volumes of orders, they are more likely to look after NS in making sure orders are fulfilled correctly and on-time.

A pro-active purchasing team would also be monitoring sales trends and stock positions. This enables them to re-order in good time, taking into account supplier lead times, ensuring dependability for the customer. This is likely to enhance reputation and customer loyalty.

Flexibility

As with most businesses it is likely that NS will not always be able to predict future stock requirements with 100% accuracy. A pro-active purchasing team will constantly be monitoring sales trends and stock levels. This can lead to constant changes in stock and supply requirements. This flexibility is needed to meet ever-changing customer needs as suggested by the Sales Manager.

In order to meet constantly changing customer needs, it is important that NS work with flexible suppliers. For example, uncertainty in demand requirements may require more deliveries from suppliers with fewer goods on each delivery. This is something that the purchasing team must recognise and arrange with suppliers.

The development of systems and information technology can help to meet these changing needs. Joint development of systems with suppliers is a critical area of supply chain management.

Flexibility in supply will mean having the right goods at the right time for customers.

Costs

All businesses need to operate at the minimum cost possible. A large element of total cost for a retail business is, obviously, the cost of their stock. Two main elements of stock cost are price and stock level. Effective supply management can reduce cost in both of these areas.

By developing long-term relationships with suppliers, and so providing some degree of assurance of future business, suppliers may be willing to offer lower prices in return.

By working with high quality, speedy, dependable and flexible supplier's stock levels can be kept to a minimum.

At the same time the costs of poor quality, customer returns, rush orders and stock-outs are minimised.

Lower costs in these areas will help NS to compete on price with the larger National chains. However, NS must be careful to balance cost against the quality of service they receive from their suppliers.

Achieving quality, flexibility and so on can cost money. Some of this cost may have to be passed on to NS through increased prices of goods. Through effective supply chain management NS should balance this potential increased price of goods against cost savings through better quality assurance, shorter lead times, increased dependability and flexibility. Thus, an increased price on goods may be worth paying as the other benefits gained can lead to more customers, good reputation and increased customer loyalty.

(c) Cousins "Strategic Supply Wheel" depicts the corporate supply strategy at the hub of a wheel. It underlines the need for an integrated approach to supply strategy involving the balancing of all of the spokes of the wheel.

The five elements of Cousins "Strategic Supply Wheel" and, therefore, the areas for the Board of NS to concentrate on are as follows:

Organisation Structure
This affects the interactions with the rest of the organisation and the way in which control is exercised. The three main options are centralised, decentralised or a "hybrid" between the two.

As NS have a chain of five shops they must decide whether purchasing will be conducted centrally by the head office, each shop will have its own purchasing function or whether certain items will be purchased centrally with the remainder purchased locally.

Relationships with Suppliers
The supplier relationship may impact on the strategic success of the organisation. These relationships may be based on driving deals on price and can be quite adversarial. Alternatively, they may be more collaborative where there is a joint quest to reduce costs and a sharing of technology and innovations.

At present NS have only one supplier. In the past it seems there may have been a successful collaborative relationship, however, since Bruce's friend left the company it seems the relationship has deteriorated. As it will be difficult for NS to compete on price with the larger National chains it may in their best interests to seek out additional suppliers with whom they can develop new collaborative relationships. This may help them to achieve some of the benefits outlined in part b.

Cost/benefit Analysis
According to Cousins, this is at the heart of rational decisions over the most strategic approach to follow.

As stated in part b, NS must strike a balance between the benefits of collaboration with suppliers (quality, speed, dependability, flexibility) and with the cost of supplies. In addition, the costs and benefits of operating a centralised or decentralised purchasing structure must also be taken into account.

Competences
Appropriate skills and competences are vital in order to implement a chosen strategy. Long-term relationships with suppliers might, for instance, lead to a need to re-orientate and train key personnel.

If NS decide to pursue a supply chain management approach there will be a need for training of personnel from all functions and levels of the organisation. New competences for multiple supplier management will also be needed.

Performance Measures
Both internal and external performance measures are needed for monitoring and control. They must be aligned with the strategy.

If NS follows a supply chain management approach they should set performance measures in the areas of quality, speed, dependability, flexibility and cost for their suppliers as a minimum. Internally, performance measures could be set for each shop if they were to be decentralised.

Summary
From a strategic point of view cohesion between the five elements of the wheel needs to be achieved with each element supporting the others.

Answer 9

Requirement (a)

As a good employer B & G will want, as far as possible, to minimise the human cost involved in achieving the job reductions. This means that the actions will need to be sensitively handled and seek to cushion negative impacts upon the individual. Such measures might be seen as "positive" initiatives. The process might be viewed as a series of steps:

- In the first instance B & G should review staff turnover rates that presently exist and determine how much of the 50% can be achieved through "natural wastage" due to normal turnover.
- B & G should also be able to project from HR records those who will reach retirement age within the next year. Natural retirement and turnover may make some inroads into the 50% target set.
- As a next step B & G should then put an embargo on further external recruitment and seek to fill vital posts short term from within.
- It should also stop any overtime and seek to spread excess work to other under-utilised employees.

B & G will need to consider and discuss possible alternatives with the relevant trade unions or staff representatives such as:

- Contracting out non-core functions (for example IT) and try to negotiate a transfer of staff to the outsourcing company.
- Encouraging those over retirement age to leave.
- Job-sharing (between two or more people?).
- A shorter working week.

Note: These final two points will not reduce absolute numbers but will impact on computated "full time equivalent" numbers.

The important thing is that any initiative is adopted in conjunction with employee groups (for example trade unions) rather than being imposed. If, as a last resort, jobs need to be made redundant, agreed processes must be followed. Attempts to find new work, including the use of outplacement consultants, might be helpful to individuals affected.

Appropriate support for individuals concerned might include:

- Counselling and support groups for those retiring early.
- Training for those with skill deficiencies in order to undertake other roles within the company.

- Counselling, financial advice and other support for those made redundant.
- Outplacement consultants and job fairs staged in order to get redundant workers back into work.

Requirement (b)

Kotter and Schlesinger (1979) identify six main strategies for dealing with resistance. This might usefully serve as a framework for discussion:

Education and communication is particularly useful when the basic problem is a lack of information about the need for, or the nature of, the planned change. The approach can be very time-consuming and will not work by itself if there are reasons other than misunderstanding leading to resistance to change. Such a strategy would seem to be appropriate in this case. As a good employer B & G is honour bound to present all known facts on the plight of the company and discuss options openly and straightforwardly. A suitable strategy.

Participation and involvement increases the chances of commitment to implementing the change particularly if their views are taken into account. This method is particularly appropriate when the people affected by the change have considerable power to resist it. This approach can be time-consuming. Such a strategy would seem to be appropriate in this case. Whatever positive measure is chosen, participation is vital to ensuring its success. The change is more acceptable if it is done by you rather than to you! A highly suitable strategy.

Facilitation and support involves training, counselling and discussions, designed to reduce anxiety. This is particularly appropriate where the principal reason for resistance is based on insecurity and adjustment problems. Such a strategy would seem to be appropriate in this case; indeed the suggestion of outplacement is an embodiment of this strategy. A highly suitable strategy.

Negotiation and agreement may be necessary to compensate those losing out because of the change. This may help avoid major problems, but it can be expensive in terms of for example redundancy packages. If there is little goodwill between the parties it may be protracted and bruising. Such a strategy would seem to be appropriate in this case, as B & G is a good employer there may be genuine goodwill between the management side and trade unions. A suitable strategy.

Manipulation and co-optation involves presenting partial or misleading information to those resisting change and "buying off" key players. This is a quick and relatively inexpensive approach, but normally results in future problems if the people involved realise they have been manipulated. Such a strategy would be inconsistent with B & G's philosophy of being a "good employer". An unsuitable strategy.

Explicit/implicit coercion involves the use of force, or the threat of force, to enforce the implementation of change. It raises ethical (and potentially legal) problems as well as involving considerable risk of making a situation more difficult, especially if trade unions are in a position to provide opposition and protection. Such a strategy would be inconsistent with B & G's philosophy of being a "good employer". An unsuitable strategy.

Answer 10

Requirement (a)

Likely role HR will perform in the light of the changing nature of the organisation:

Company Background
The company appears to be "traditionally" structured with four divisions and a small HQ staff. The signals for change include a re-branding of Personnel as Human Resources. The retirement of the long serving head of this function is also of significance. This implies that a traditional well established way of operating in the past is not required in the future. The fact that the HR strategy is in "urgent need" of review and revision underlines this point.

An HR rather than Personnel role
Personnel Management is seen as focusing on day-to-day "people related" issues. In the past NS's small specialist personnel support function would undoubtedly have attempted to ensure consistency and fairness of treatment throughout the organisation. Personnel Management is seen as ensuring compliance with organisational procedures as well as reacting and responding to external environmental changes (including employment legislation and labour market conditions). The changes taking place at NS mean that the function will have different objectives more easily identified as human resource management (HRM).

A strategic role
The new function would be expected to view employees in a different, more strategic way. A reasonable revised focus would be upon the long-term development of human resources in such a way as to deliver the strategic aspirations of the company (that is to achieve continuous improvement). The specialist HR division should provide support to Divisional Directors and other managers in order to meet detailed organisational objectives.

The new HR function would be expected to have key inputs into the strategic deliberations that are apparently underway including the setting of clear objectives. The HR Division will now be expected to shape and deliver strategies.

A training needs role
NS's new corporate initiative of continuous improvement through empowerment is of major significance for the HR Division. Under the initiative people are seen as crucial, exercising skills of thinking, challenging, innovating and implementing. The function will need to ensure that the workforce has these skills.

Empowerment involves passing power downwards for staff "closer to the action" to be responsible for making decisions and initiating actions. This involves a high degree of trust in the workforce and less directive, authoritarian control from management. This new management style means that Departmental Directors and managers will need to be encouraged by the function to make this change.

A role in cultural shaping
NS's initiative of an empowered workforce normally involves a major organisational cultural change. There is no evidence from the scenario as to how this is to be brought about other than an apparent rethink of the role of the specialist personnel function. The HR function will be crucial in effecting the necessary cultural change and the new Head might be expected to perform a change agent's role.

A role in championing corporate initiatives
In an empowered organisation, people are active in solving problems, looking for better ways of working and co-operating freely with others in and across teams. Continuous improvement is a collective approach towards improving performance throughout the organisation. Clearly the HR function will need to champion and support these developments.

Requirement (b)

Aspects of HR strategy showing significant change given the nature of recent developments. Given the changing nature of the organisation and the initiatives being progressed attention should be given to the following aspects of the HR strategy:

Structure and job roles
The overall structure should be configured in order that individuals are developed to their full potential and encouraged to do "things right" (what needs to be done in organisational terms), not merely "the right things" (what job descriptions require of them). The strategy will need to articulate the structure, control and functioning of the organisation. Layers of management that add no value or that damage empowerment should be eliminated as part of the systematic review.

Job content
Job content will also need to be reviewed and then be articulated in overall terms in the strategy. This review could conveniently follow on from the structural review identified earlier and might feature broader spans of managerial control. This should in turn encourage managers to delegate and trust subordinates to exercise increased autonomy and power effectively.

Education and Training
Education and Training in empowerment and continuous improvement will be vital components of the strategy. This might be achieved by facilitating workshops and ongoing support mechanisms such as mentors, buddying systems and/or counsellors. Changes to role require training at all levels, particularly senior management, where individuals will need to be persuaded to relinquish power. For "front line" staff, mechanisms for training and building self confidence are vital. This will undoubtedly involve enhancing existing skills and the identification of new skill requirements.

It is good practice to undertake a training needs analysis of the workforce and shape the strategy accordingly. Specific likely skills will include problem solving, data gathering techniques, team building, listening and customer care. Teams of people will need to be built that co-operate and support one another in continuously improving customer service and improving efficiency.

Senior managers may need training in facilitation and leadership skills. It is vital that senior managers (whose role should include setting the "right" examples) provide consistent messages and behaviour.

The strategy will need to articulate how this is delivered (whether in-house by trainers, externally, or by the use of existing managers). Systems for monitoring the effectiveness of these "interventions" will also need to be articulated in the strategy.

Reward systems
These systems represent the ways in which staff are recognised and rewarded for their endeavours. A revised strategy must ensure that such systems are consistent with, and encourage, the identified concepts of empowerment and continuous improvement. The HR function in conjunction with senior managers will need to agree behaviour patterns required in the future and ways of measuring outcomes. Those who actively support and embrace the twin concepts identified (of empowerment and continuous improvement) should be rewarded appropriately. Typical organisational rewards usually include pay, promotion and other rewards. Other rewards need not have financial implications and

might, for instance, include still greater empowerment. It is a good idea to communicate these points widely and reward publicly, making role models and heroes of those who achieve. In this way, positive performance standards might be signalled. This thinking should be embodied in the HR strategy.

Target setting and appraisals
A mechanism for review and target setting will need to be considered in the strategy. Although this might already exist, major revisions to these targets will be needed in the light of organisational initiatives. New personal plans/targets/key performance indicators (KPIs) will need to be created for every manager and then cascaded down through subordinates and work groups so that the whole organisation's performance is assessed having regards to the twin initiatives. Reviews of performance after a few months by using small groups should highlight progress, problems and areas for adjustment. Once overall review mechanisms are established, annual appraisal and monthly target setting might reasonably be employed. Upward and 360 degree appraisal schemes might be considered in order to strengthen reflective practice.

Review mechanisms
Revised review mechanisms should concentrate on monitoring progress on the initiatives and taking corrective action where necessary. This should be at the expense of previous forms of control, direction and reporting in order to drive decision making down to the lowest level.

Communication systems
Channels of official communication should be articulated in the strategy. The existing strategy may already do this but the focus may need to be re-orientated in the light of new corporate initiatives. A new emphasis should be placed upon encouraging open communication, sharing of information and honesty.

Answer 11

Requirement (a)

One structure for identifying main immediate marketing issues is the "Ps" framework. These issues will need to be addressed in the marketing action plan. Candidates are advised to consider only product, place and promotion.

Product
There do not appear to be any plans to expand the product range (currently fresh "quality" sandwiches, home baked snacks, "real" coffee and freshly squeezed fruit juices). One key issue is the maintenance of quality, which is vital to the company's reputation. The new technology proposed in preparing and packaging should be a timesaver and should help achieve consistency of standard. It might be helpful in the marketing action plan to identify the need to articulate product standards and procedures.

Place
Petrol filling stations apparently currently represent the organisation's sole distribution outlets. The proposal that there is potential for stocking its products in newspaper shops and railway stations represents a form of market development. However, the method proposed of extending "place" in this way is rather more questionable. Much depends on the effectiveness of drivers, and a reliance on them to perform this task is perhaps ambitious. Nevertheless, the marketing action plan will need to identify precise targets and commit training resources towards this aim. Additional time will need to be allocated to

drivers' rounds in order to perform their expanded duties and projected additional new locations will need to be factored into revised driving rounds. This may necessitate the use of extra vehicles and this should also be articulated in the plan.

Promotion
Local radio advertising appears to be successful in expanding operations so far. The growth strategy until now has been based on "more of the same" and repeat purchases. The use of drivers to cement existing sales relationships is a sensible policy but the effectiveness of using "cold call" selling is (according to conventional wisdom) questionable. The action plan will need to attach SMART targets to these aspirations (specific, measurable, attainable, realistic, time bound) and quantity the amounts that will be spent on radio advertising as well as the time allocated to "cold calling" by drivers.

Requirement (b)

The job description
The job description defines the job: its overall purpose and the main tasks to be carried out. These aspects are reflected in the following draft:

Draft Job Description:

Company Delivery and Customer Interface Department

Job title: Permanent Driver

Responsible to: Head of Delivery and Customer Relations

Posts responsible to the jobholder: None

Brief description and overall purpose
The purpose of the job is to load a delivery vehicle at the depot and make timely deliveries of company products to the locations listed on the delivery round throughout the day.

The post requires finding the customer's location, dealing with relevant paperwork, talking to customer's employees, and reporting back.

The post holder will be required to get direct feedback from customers, and liaise with outlet personnel to:

- Ascertain customer perceptions.
- Discuss possibilities for taking new product lines and likely future demand.
- Gain information on competitor's products.

The post holder will also be required to discuss the possibility of stocking company products at other outlets that are located on or near the delivery round.

The post holder will be required to complete simple computerised daily returns to the Head of Delivery and Customer Relations based on interactions with customers, outlets and potential outlets.

Technical procedures/tools/machinery/equipment used:
The post holder will be required to drive a delivery vehicle.

The post holder will be required to use a laptop computer (provided) to complete daily reports.

Special requirements to deal with outside contacts:
The post holder will be required to maintain a good working relationship with existing outlet staff and agree delivery quantities.

The post holder will be required to liaise with customers, existing outlet staff and potential outlet staff.

Physical location of job and travelling required:
The post holder will be based at the company depot but required to complete delivery rounds specified on a daily basis.

Special circumstances:
Products are delivered throughout the day. The post holder will be required to complete an 8 hour shift. The post holder may be required to work overtime/or weekends dependent upon the overall requirements of the department.

The post holder will be required to lift and carry relatively lightweight loads as part of the delivery pattern.

Other responsibilities:
The post holder will be required to complete basic paperwork.

There will be no budgetary responsibility.

Miscellaneous:
Terms and conditions of employment including salary, details of shifts and holiday entitlement are embodied separately in the post holder's letter of appointment.

Answer 12

(a) Organisational Development (OD) is an umbrella term used most frequently to describe methods or techniques for improving the health of the whole organisation. It emerged as a distinct approach in the 1960s and is usually associated with the work of a number of social scientists. Bennis defined the approach more precisely as:

> a response to change, a complex educational strategy intended to change the beliefs, attitudes, values and structure of an organisation so that it can better adapt to new technologies, markets and challenges and the dizzying rate of change itself.

Given its origin in the United States, it is not surprising to find that the underlying values of OD are humanistic and democratic. People undertaking the task of OD tend to assume that the best way to tackle problems such as conflicts between individuals or between work groups is to confront them openly. Collaborative and participative processes and a spirit of enquiry are also seen as essential to the successful development of a healthy organisation.

The use of OD in organisations normally commences with a period of investigation in the form of some kind of survey or piece of action research before any one of a number of other separate interventions are undertaken to tackle the underlying problems. For example, some form of action research may be conducted to see what happens, if counselling some section of the workforce reduces tension in that part of the organisation. Such an effect may then encourage the wider use of counselling in other parts of the organisation. Since action research involves interventions as the research proceeds, it follows that developments may occur in an emergent less tidy manner than under a conventional planning approach which only implements changes when the research has been completed.

Examples of how OD has been used for organisational improvement can be found in large companies like British Telecom and British Airways (BA) and huge projects like the American Space programme.

In British Telecom, OD techniques that include regular climate surveys, team-building, objective-setting, skill development, inter-divisional problem-solving forums and communication and employee involvement programmes have been used to improve the quality of service to customers following the large-scale impact of privatisation, liberalisation and technological change in the telecoms industry.

Following deregulation and privatisation, BA also made use of OD techniques to move BA from a subsidised government-owned bureaucratic organisation to a privately owned entrepreneurial company that was then able to market itself as "The World's Favourite Airline."

Organisational Development techniques employed to facilitate these changes included experiential programmes that involved heavy doses of individual feedback to managers about their behaviour regarding management practices on the job. The overall purpose of such programmes was to identify the existing dysfunctional management style and to develop a new management style that would fit BA's new competitive environment. Redefining BA as a service business rather than one simply of transportation also required a critical shift on the level of climate/interpersonal style because a service business needs an open climate and good interpersonal skills combined with good teamwork. This was achieved through off-site team-building and skill training sessions. Other OD techniques employed by BA included process consultation which involved the consultant examining BA's patterns of communication. This was achieved through a combination of direct observation of staff meetings and by raising questions and making observations about communications between individuals. The overall intent was to expose hidden agendas and to create a more open and frank exchange between members of staff.

One of the most well-known and widespread uses of the approach arose in the aerospace industry in the USA. During this programme, specialists from variety of backgrounds often had difficulty in working together. In order to overcome this problem, OD consultants used T-groups (therapy groups) and confrontation meetings to help improve relationships. Essentially, these involved small unstructured groups within which participants were encouraged to explore their own feelings and relationships with others: successful groups would then move on to determine more effective ways of working together.

A key feature of OD is usually the involvement of an independent "third party" as facilitator for the change. He or she will act as a catalyst for the process by acting as a change agent who helps members of the organisation to diagnose the underlying problems, resolve conflicts and implement effective change. As part of the initial diagnosis, this third party will often carry out some initial survey of existing attitudes, which will be fed back to all parties involved in the change process.

In the early days of OD, the key techniques consisted of a limited number such as process consultation, survey feedback, conflict resolution and team development but as time has gone on, different consultants and writers have added their favourite techniques so that the list of possible techniques is now a long one.

(b) As already indicated in answer to requirement (a), the list of possible methods and techniques that could be used to assist in the diagnosis and treatment of the B

Company is now very broad and includes coaching and counselling, team-building, inter-group activities, training and development, role analysis, job redesign/job enrichment/enlargement, questionnaires, surveys, interviews, action research, group meetings, planning/objectives-setting/decision-making, process consultation and Business Process Re-engineering.

To determine which of the techniques are most useful for helping to overcome the B Company's problems, it will help to begin with the problems described. Some of these problems are external to the B Company and are things that the Company will be forced to react to, rather than things that can be changed. This is particularly true of the new hygiene regulations, changes in consumer tastes, rising material costs and increasing competition. Pay demands from staff may be a manifestation of dissatisfaction amongst staff but could equally well be due to external factors like a cost of living increase.

What OD can assist with are the problems affecting staff including those of low morale, conflict between departments, lack of confidence in management and the feeling that the organisation has lost its direction.

One technique that may usefully be applied early on in the investigation of the B Company's problems is the 'survey feedback' technique. In this, the results of an employee survey are fed back to managers and employees to help in identifying action that will improve organisational effectiveness. Surveys may include questions on leadership and management style, communications, motivation and morale and member satisfaction along with other aspects of the organisation.

These findings can then be used to encourage discussion about ways to resolve differences and solve the problems identified. The most popular approach for achieving this is through group discussions, be these task forces, working parties or project teams. Each of these may work on a particular set of themes or issues, or direct their attention to a particular section of the organisation. By this means, the underlying reasons for low morale and lack of confidence in the management in the B Company might well be revealed.

Allied to survey feedback and complementing it is the method of "process consultation". This usually involves the hiring of an external consultant in an advisory role, to help individuals to improve their understanding of organisational problems, and to identify problem-solving actions. The role of the process consultant would be to help managers in the B Company to develop an insight into the reasons or causes of the problems they face. This requires a great deal of skill, sensitivity and tact and there are no standard procedures to follow. The critical skills for a process consultant are in diagnosis, and in forming a supportive, helping relationship. The diagnostic and problem-solving activities of the process consultant are, by definition, joint activities, carried out with the client or clients and not for the client. The focus is on process, which explains the label. Process consultation contrasts with the conventional view of the consultant as an "expert", where the client is buying specific knowledge and expertise to cover gaps in the organisation and also to address and resolve a particular problem.

Given the potentially wide nature of the support offered by the process consultant, it follows that it is not easy to pick out specific problems experienced by the B Company. Any or all the internal problems mentioned could potentially gain from assistance given by the process consultant.

Moving from the investigatory stages of OD to tackling the problems themselves, we find a number of techniques that might aid the members of the B Company resolve their problems. First comes "sensitivity training" – sometimes called T-group training. This is a situation in which the OD specialist sets up T-groups and then acts as facilitator in an educational process, that helps individuals to develop trust and confidence in each other as they learn to express their feelings and attitudes openly. In this way, interpersonal barriers to working together as an effective team may be substantially reduced. Training in team working may, of course, offer similar benefits depending on how this process is carried out.

In conflict resolution, the OD specialist's strategy is to organise situations in which the conflicting parties are brought together in open confrontation. By such means, it is hoped to clarify misunderstanding and to provide a basis for collaboration in the future. Clearly this would be very useful if it could be employed successfully in the case of the B Company where we see that there is conflict between, at least, two departments.

The feeling amongst staff that the B Company has lost direction could be improved by joint exercises on planning/objective-setting in which managers and employees are involved in discussions about the future of the company and their particular role in contributing to this future. Having a clear idea of one's objectives and of the means to achieve these is known to have motivational benefits and may also help lift morale in the Company.

Answer 13

(a) The traditional idea of training involves the learning of specific skills. For example, the retail assistants in the D retail store must be capable of answering customers' requests for information about such things as products, sizes and styles. Similarly the check-out assistants must have the skills necessary to work the tills efficiently and direct customer complaints or returns to the relevant persons within the store. The concern of the Store Manager is therefore with ensuring that employees have specific skills to ensure that the objectives of her department can be fulfilled. In the case of simple tasks like packaging the pottery, it is probably relatively easy to learn the skills on-the-job itself, either by copying what others do and/or by watching a demonstration and listening to specific instructions before practising the task oneself.

By contrast, the HR Manager's notion of employee development is not only concerned with the possession of skills to do the present job to a certain standard; but is also concerned with the preparation of staff members for future roles in the organisation and/or for doing existing tasks/jobs to a higher standard. So development is concerned with preparation for higher-level roles in the organisation. It is concerned with enabling individuals to grow in skills and experience. This growth might take place through deliberate efforts on the part of the organisation through a series of well-structured programmes or experiences or it may be through the efforts of the individual who deliberately seeks out development opportunities of an informal or formal kind, be these inside or outside their place of work.

(b) The concept of "a learning organisation" is a step beyond the individual learning that training and development is generally concerned with. It really relates to a collective learning that encompasses not only the learning of individual employees but continually adds to the organisation's reservoir of knowledge and competences.

The concept of the learning organisation encompasses a range of ideas drawn from a number of sources. Among these, the following are generally acknowledged as being important aspects.

First, the learning organisation is regarded as a process rather than a product. The emphasis is on continuous learning rather than a particular end-state of knowledge because rapid change demands new ways of doing things, and new skills and knowledge to enable the organisation to compete.

Second, the learning organisation does not come in turnkey form. In other words, it is not simply a matter of installing it like a piece of equipment, as it is a continuous process of learning that involves everyone in the organisation on an ongoing basis.

Third, it is different from simply the summation of the learning of individuals in an organisation. Though organisations do not have brains, they have cognitive systems and memories that preserve certain behaviours, mental maps, norms and values over time. Individuals may come and go but provided that their learning has been passed on to others in the organisation, the benefit of their learning to the organisation continues.

Fourth, only when individual learning has an impact on, and interrelates with others do organisation members learn together and gradually begin to change how things are done. This increases collective competence as well as individual competence.

Some writers also argue that the learning organisation involves "double-loop learning". The process seeks to correct errors by going right back to the underlying policies and values in the decision-making process to establish whether the taken-for-granted rules under which the organisation operates are in fact appropriate for effective decisions. This contrasts with the more usual approach of single-loop learning whereby organisations simply seek to solve problems and correct errors by changing routine behaviour, rather than examining the assumptions and policies on which it is based.

The notion of organisational learning has been elaborated on by a number of writers, including Senge, Argyris and Schon and Pedlar.

Among these writers, the ideas of Senge have received most attention. Senge suggests that the evolution of learning organisations can be understood as a series of three waves. If Senge's prescriptions are correct, then the HR Manager in the D Company can help it become a learning organisation by use of the following waves or phased activities.

The *first wave* is primarily concerned with frontline workers, and management's task is to:

- champion continual improvement;
- remove bureaucratic barriers to improvement; and
- support initiatives such as benchmarking and quality training that drive process improvements.

The *second wave* is concerned with encouraging new ways of thinking about how organisational processes such as manufacturing and customer satisfaction interact with each other. During this stage the primary focus of change is on the managers themselves.

The *third wave* is one in which "learning becomes institutionalised as an inescapable way of life, for managers and workers". By this, Senge is talking about how learning can be ingrained as a way of life for the workforce. Presumably such learning would need to be continually reinforced by all manner of means such as encouragement, training and development courses, on-the-job learning, the use of incentives and so on.

More particularly, the HR Manager could help the D Company to become a learning organisation by encouraging the following developments in the company which Senge argues are necessary for a learning organisation to fully evolve:

1 *Building a shared vision*: It is necessary to ensure that people are focused around a common set of values, rather than learning only when there is a crisis that brings everyone temporarily together.
2 *Personal mastery*: Senge grounds this idea in the familiar competencies and skills associated with management but it also includes spiritual growth – opening oneself up to a progressively deeper reality – and living life from a creative, rather than a reactive viewpoint. This discipline involves two underlying movements – continually learning how to see current reality more clearly, and understanding how the ensuing gap between vision and reality produces the creative tension from which learning arises.
3 *Working with mental models*: This is one way for people to recognise their unconscious assumptions, and to appreciate how alternative actions at work could create a different reality. For example, the Japanese development of JIT is an example of how alternative ways of doing things are possible.
4 *Team learning*: A learning organisation requires individuals to come together and act as a team, so that it can be practised when groups of people have to confront controversial issues and make difficult decisions.
5 *Systems thinking*: This emphasises the importance of understanding interrelationships, rather than breaking problems down into discrete parts. In practical terms, this can help managers spot repetitive patterns, such as the way certain kinds of problems persist, or the way systems have their own in-built limits to growth.

Pedlar and his co-authors take a different line and, rather than saying directly how to create a learning organisation, they seek to identify a series of characteristics which they argue are significant in creating the learning environment. The HR Manager, they would argue needs to:

- encourage a much wider debate on strategy and policy formation;
- create an environment where tensions are welcomed as they can precede creative solutions to problems that were previously seen as "win-lose" resolutions of difficulties;
- "informat", that is, use information technology to inform and empower for the many rather than for the few;
- encourage the exchange of information – getting closer to internal and external customers and suppliers;
- use the people who meet the external customers to bring back useful information about needs and opportunities;
- collaborate rather than compete and make use of internal and external best-practice comparisons;
- encourage self-development opportunities for everyone in the organisation;
- encourage individuals to take responsibility for their own learning and development.

Answer 14

(a) (i) For any organisation like S Company, the growth and diversification of the business poses an increasing problem of control. As the number of levels in the organisation is increased and the number of different kinds of tasks to be carried out multiplies, the division of labour becomes more complex. In this changing situation, it becomes increasingly difficult to ensure that members of an organisation are doing what they are supposed to be doing.

Without some attempt to control what people do in organisations, there is a danger of centrifugal tendencies developing – that is, people begin, intentionally or unintentionally, to do "their own thing" by working towards their own personal goals and perceived self-interests. To counteract the tendencies created by the processes of differentiation, and to ensure goal congruence, there is a need to create a "common focus" in an organisation, which will control and integrate members' diverse activities. This is why organisations introduce a variety of formal controls.

In small, simple organisations it is possible for the owner/manager or senior management to supervise subordinates' activities personally and systematically. Often, in such organisations, it is possible to achieve control in an informal way by setting employees tasks and then checking that they have been carried out. Any deviations from the accepted standard of performance can be communicated directly by the owner/manager to particular employees and the necessary corrective action taken. In larger organisations, however, with a complex division of labour, and a taller hierarchy of responsibility, it is not physically possible to control people in such a simple manner. In such situations, formal policies, rules and procedures have to be put into place together with a system of rewards and punishments to ensure that the policies, rules and procedures are observed.

In such hierarchical organisations, policies and objectives are typically set, or at least confirmed, by occupants of higher-level positions and are then communicated to lower-level staff, who are then charged with the responsibility to carry out the necessary actions. It is up to the higher-level managers to determine whether or not the objectives have been met and, if not, to take the appropriate steps. This is the process of control.

It is important to note, however, that there are a number of different ways of exercising control in organisations and that the effectiveness of a particular type of control system depends on a number of factors including the organisations's strategy, culture, structure, environment and the type of goods or services produced.

In the case of S Company, it chose to use bureaucratic (administrative) forms of control, but as the CEO realised, such a form of control is not conducive to creativity and innovation.

(ii) Creativity can be defined as "the generation of new ideas, and innovation, which is the transformation of creative ideas into tangible products or processes" varies considerably between one organisation and another. Some organisations, like 3M, Hewlett Packard and Microsoft have a reputation for creativity and innovation while other organisations hardly ever seem to generate new products or new ways of doing things.

The generation of new ideas and their translation into commercial use is a particularly important issue for an organisation like S Company because its future depends on a continuous supply of innovative software products.

There are many factors influencing the rate of innovation in organisations, but research suggests that one reason has to do with how an organisation is structured and controlled. Studies by Rosabeth Moss Kanter and others have found that excessive bureaucracy with its allegiance to central control and to rules and procedures discourages creativity and innovation. The focus on rules and procedures and the accompanying sanctions designed to ensure compliance means that employees "play safe" by sticking to the rules rather than risk trying out new ideas. As R. K. Merton pointed out, rules become "ends in themselves".

The division of labour that often accompanies the growth of an organisation also affects creativity and innovation because it restricts the sharing of ideas between individuals and between different units, departments or divisions.

The case of S Company illustrates well the problems faced by all large organisations at some time in their development: that of balancing the need to ensure adequate direction and control of staff and yet allowing sufficient freedom and discretion of middle managers and other employees to contribute their particular knowledge and expertise to the organisation. Too little direction and control can result in wasted effort and inefficiencies as the departments and divisions into which an organisation is sub-divided pursue their own particular goals; too much central control can make lower-level staff frustrated by rules and procedures forced upon them from the higher level by those who are too far from the action to make informed decisions.

(b) The most important means to help balance control with autonomy and so encourage creativity and innovation is through the related processes of decentralisation, delegation and empowerment. Decentralisation involves specific delegation of authority for decision-making within certain limits to sub-units of S Company such as strategic business units, divisions or departments. Delegation refers to the conferring of specified authority to individuals by a higher authority and empowerment is similar to delegation in that it allows greater freedom, autonomy and self-control to teams and/or individuals, but responsibility is also devolved.

All these related processes have in common the idea that organisational sub-units and/or particular individual post-holders have discretion to make decisions and to act within the limits agreed by those higher in the organisation's chain of command. The autonomy granted to units and individuals through these processes contributes to creativity and innovation because it allows people with specialised knowledge and skill the freedom to pursue their own ideas for improved products and processes.

The problem for the organisation is, as already noted, that of ensuring that employees keep within the bounds of their authority and use their time and other company resources in ways that contribute to the organisation's overall objectives. This brings us back to the means by which organisational members can best be controlled.

Three main forms of internal organisational control have been identified: bureaucratic control, output control and cultural control. S Company appears to have adopted bureaucratic forms of control, but as we have seen, these are not conducive to an organisation that depends on a continuous flow of innovative new software for its survival.

The use of output forms of control may provide an answer to S Company's problem if the output in terms of creativity and innovation could be measured. Output control strategy is aimed at facilitating the delegation of operational decision-making without the need for bureaucratic controls or close supervision. The problem for S Company, however, is likely to be that of setting measures for creativity and innovation.

Perhaps therefore a form of cultural control will be of more use. The basis of cultural control is the willing compliance of employees with management requirements. This, in turn, requires an acceptance of the values and beliefs or the organisation and its objectives. The implementation of cultural control would require a careful selection, socialisation and training of staff to ensure commitment to the objective of continuous innovation. Once commitment to objectives has been achieved via these methods, semi-autonomous methods of working could be introduced with the use of self-managing teams with responsibility for completing particular software development projects. The use of financial incentives can also be used to support systems of cultural control.

Other means to assist innovation include "internal new venturing", which is a form of entrepreneurship. The idea is to design organisations to encourage creativity and give new-venture managers the opportunity and resources to develop new products or markets. To provide a new-venture unit that gives managers the autonomy to experiment and take risks, the company sets up a new-venture division separate from other divisions and makes it a centre for new product or project development. Away from the day-to-day scrutiny of top management, divisional staff pursue the creation of new products as though they were external entrepreneurs. The division is operated by controls that reinforce the entrepreneurial spirit. Bureaucratic and output controls are seen as inappropriate because they can inhibit risk-taking. Instead, the company develops a culture for entrepreneurship in the new-venture division to provide a climate for innovation. Care must be taken, however, to institute some bureaucratic controls that put some limits on freedom of action. Otherwise, costly mistakes may be made, and resources wasted.

Answer 15

(a) The key mistakes made by the CEO in initiating the change programme in B Company were as follows:

- He did not involve the rest of the management team or other staff in discussion of the company's problems and what needed to be done to resolve these. In other words, there was a complete lack of participation.
- Using email to inform staff of such important changes is inappropriate for communicating a change programme of this magnitude for the company.
- Delegation of change management to the Head of HR is questionable. For such important developments, the CEO or perhaps some management consultant may have been more appropriate to drive the change programme.
- No specific plans were set out for how changes were to be implemented.
- No allocation of extra time and resources were provided to conduct the change.
- No sensitivity or awareness has been demonstrated as to how the changes would affect his staff.
- Rather naïve assumptions have been made about the problems of cultural change.

- Possibly conflicting objectives such as that between controlling costs and encouragement of an entrepreneurial culture.
- The CEO was not available to answer questions or respond to concerns that staff may have following the announcement.

(b) To ensure that the changes are successfully implemented, the CEO will need to start again. This will involve:

- An early meeting with heads of departments to explain to them the results of the benchmarking exercise and the gap between the company's performance and that of the key competitors. He will need to elaborate on his ideas for the changes that he has suggested and to ask for their ideas on these suggestions. This may involve a series of working parties to consider how best such changes could be accomplished.
- As part of his initial briefing he would also need to reassure heads of functional departments, if possible, that their salaries would be protected in any event and that all of them would be given fair consideration in the re-structuring programme towards a divisional structure.
- Working with his subordinates on specific plans for undertaking the change.
- The CEO will need to agree with his senior staff, a set of priorities as to which part of the change programme should be undertaken first.
- He will also have to ensure that sufficient time and resources are available to put the changes into effect. The organisation will have to continue to function during the period when the changes are implemented.
- Such changes also have training and development implications, so provision will have to be made to ensure that people taking on new roles are adequately equipped to cope.
- The changes are so extensive that there will inevitably be knock-on effects on other systems and procedures. For instance, a change of organisation structure will probably require re-alignment of the management information and reporting system. In fact, a working party could usefully be convened to look into the wider implications of the changes being proposed.
- The CEO would be well advised to seek advice on introducing cultural change. Research has shown that this is a slow and difficult process, that it can take a considerable time and that it needs constant re-enforcement. Cultural change has implications for a range of organisational systems and policies.

Answer 16

(a) *Dangers to Everland banks if they do not change*. Product-orientated organisations, like Everland banks, have a main focus of product (or service) features. This does not necessarily imply that Everland banks are offering shoddy services, indeed they concentrate their attention on the services they offer. The danger is more that such offerings are unsupported by research of the market's needs or by deep understanding of what customers want and in what quantity. Services are therefore a result of intuition, trial and error and may not match demand. This is an inefficient method of operating.

The biggest threat to Everland banks is the complacency they exhibits in the light of an external environment that is about to change radically.

If banks within Everland do not become marketing orientated there are clear dangers, mainly that they will lose out to much more effective new competitors.

There are presently only a few banks operating in Everland, and these enjoy an oligopoly-type position. The difficulty is that this protection has apparently led banks to be complacent and failing to innovate their portfolio of services. As a consequence, customers may well be frustrated by the limitations of these services. The anticipated increased competition may be too hard to handle now that new legislation has opened up the market to competition by international players and other financial institutions. These institutions are likely to have a broader experience of customer orientation and diversity of management skills than that currently exhibited by Everland's banking industry.

Unless Everland banks reform quickly and change their philosophy away from the present product orientation, more customer-focused rivals may be driving them out of business. (The emerging use of cross national online banking and the experience of Utopia banks may ideally suit them to competing for market share in Everland, for instance.)

Lessons from Utopia
A marketing philosophy similarly to that being pursued in Utopia places customers at the heart of all organisational activities and focuses on satisfying customers' needs and wants. These "market orientated" banks put customer needs first and provide services that meet their needs. Market-orientated organisations have a main focus of customers and their demands. The benefit is that the services offered are determined by customer demands.

Emerging trends
The evidence of Utopia is that customers are becoming more demanding and that vital marketing thinking and techniques are needed to meet these demands. If customers in Utopia feel this way then this is also a likely trend in Everland. The danger of Everland banks not changing is that they will not fulfil customer demands in the same way that new competitors may be able to.

(b) Types of change that banks should be making in order to survive and prosper.

Changes required

Some of the change which the adoption of marketing concepts and techniques in the banking sector could give rise to are included in the listing below:

Techniques:

- Greater market research and analysis in order to keep abreast of customer needs.
- More sophisticated monitoring of levels of customers' satisfaction.
- More effective marketing planning emphasising techniques such as market segmentation.

Structure:

- Marketing expertise elevated to the position of providing a strategic co-ordinating role for the resources and activities of the business.

- Organisational restructuring based around customer and market requirements. This might for example involve a structure based on products and market segments.
- New marketing style positions at the expense of traditional banking roles.

Skills:

- New specialist skills such as "brand managers" and "market analysts" may be seen as vital. These may be fundamental to a revised organisational structure.

Systems:

- More effective marketing control and feedback systems.
- An increased emphasis on quality, service and customer care.
- Maximising use of some of technology in marketing in order to (for example) support relationship marketing with customers.
- Systems that provide awareness of wider environmental forces and enhanced recognition of ethical and social responsibilities towards customers.

HR policies

- Effective HR policies such as recruitment and training are necessary in order to equip the workforce with the necessary skill mix. This is to remedy the position of senior management of commercial banks coming from a banking background and possessing few, if any, marketing and HR skills.

Answer 17

(a) The initiatives identified using Herzberg's motivation-hygiene (dual factor) theory as a framework.

The first initiative involves a revision of the system that measures managerial accountability (now on net profit rather than increasing turnover). The second involves a restructure and reallocation of duties giving SBUs greater control over their own performance.

This thinking can be explained within the context of Frederick Herzberg's motivation-hygiene, or dual factor, theory. Herzberg's contention was that the opposite of job satisfaction is the *absence of job satisfaction* and not *job dissatisfaction*. By extension, the opposite of *job dissatisfaction* is an *absence of dissatisfaction*. Herzberg's research indicated that satisfaction and dissatisfaction are influenced and created by different variables. His theory has been very influential across a wide range of jobs, organisations and countries.

His initial study in the 1950s of 203 Pittsburgh accountants and engineers focused on when they felt either exceptionally good or exceptionally bad about their job. This ultimately led to a two-factor theory of motivation:

- Motivators (or satisfiers) are factors that if present within a job encourage individuals to greater effort and performance through higher levels of job satisfaction (but not dissatisfaction). These factors relate to what people are allowed to do and the quality of human experience at work. These are the variables that motivate people. Examples include job role, organisational recognition, personal growth and a sense of achievement, advancement and responsibility. These factors are said to relate to job content.

- Hygiene factors (or dissatisfiers) are factors including status, pay, interpersonal relations, supervision, organisational policy and administration, job security and working conditions. These factors relate to job context.

In this case both motivators and hygiene factors have been addressed as follows:

Motivators

- Achievement of individual "performance contracts".
- Recognition by the chief executive of the vital role played by SBU managers.
- Promises of advancement by fast tracking to senior positions.
- Greater responsibility to get on with the real job.
- Greater autonomy and influence over the SBU managers' own "bottom-line" performance.

Hygiene factors

- New remuneration package reflecting bonuses for increased profitability.
- Organisational policy and administration adjusted with SBU managers in mind.
- Potential to improve working conditions as managers are given greater freedom to run their SBU in the way they see most appropriate.

Both of the initiatives, therefore, go to the heart of motivation and performance. Measurements of performance within someone's control against corporate objectives such as with CQ4 can in themselves be powerful means of positively influencing individuals. There is also a well-researched connection between reward and performance. The way in which the remuneration package is adjusted therefore is crucial in this respect.

(b) Factors that should be taken into account by HR department when redesigning the remuneration and reward package for SBU managers:

- *Control of total payroll costs*: CQ4 needs to decide how much overall it can afford in payroll costs. Once the costs associated with other groups are calculated then the overall base salary costs and bonus payments for managers can be determined.
- *Appropriateness of overall package*: The remuneration strategy needs to appropriately balance base and performance related pay. The base pay element should recognise factors such as size of SBU, relative contribution to the company as a whole, and specific skills and competences demanded of the individual manager and so on. The reward package will need to address not only internal targets, but also market place levels of reward for similar work in order that there are not problems associated with retention of staff. As CQ4 is a European operation it is likely that local pay rates will vary enormously between countries in which SBUs are situated.
- *Money available for performance-related pay*: Performance-related pay represents an attempt to establish closer links between results and rewards. The success of the chief executive's new initiatives is dependent on people, primarily managers, behaving in certain ways. Rewards should be directed towards those who adopt the behaviours required. The incentive of performance-related pay should be seen as no less generous than the previous bonus scheme, and sufficient to make managers innovate, risk take and improve bottom line performance. HR professionals need to know the total amount available to finance the new scheme. Based on this, decisions can be made as to how the scheme can be implemented (whether as a percentage of basic pay, a percentage of net profit, or incremental flat rate payments and so on).

- *Rewards encouraging risk taking and innovation*: The new chief executive's vision of risk taking and innovation when translated into reward systems can be problematic. Whilst precise quantitative measures are readily available to measure net profit, the other factors suggest difficulties in identification and measurement. Judgements on, for instance, the number and quality of initiatives taken may lead to feelings of unfairness. In addition there needs to be a shared understanding of the relative weighting given to profitability, risk taking and innovation. Appropriate metrics and evaluation criteria need to be agreed upon and put in place.
- *Impact of adjusted HR policies on other groups*: SBU managers are the main focus of remuneration and reward systems. This can present some difficulties, as it is probable that others (for example directors, SBU workforce) will also be involved in achieving the level of SBU performance. If the manager is perceived to be receiving unfair reward and recognition, this might have a negative impact on these other groups and may lead to workplace disharmony and endanger improved performance. The positive impact of work groups on individual motivation has long been recognised and was famously illustrated by the Hawthorne Studies. The new reward system should not, therefore, be seen as a cause of undermining teamwork within SBUs. It is likely that HR policies will also need to be reviewed for all other groups to prevent this happening.
- *Accounting for non-controllable factors that influence managerial performance*: An underlying philosophy of performance-related pay should be to provide a fair and consistent basis for rewarding managerial performance. However, other organisational factors, such as the availability of technology, raw materials and financial resources will also have an important effect on SBU performance. Consideration needs to be given as to how to account for these factors.
- *Translating longer-term objectives into short-term targets and rewards*: Strategic objectives such as those expressed by the chief executive are longer term, but managers need shorter term targets and rewards. Careful development of individual "performance contracts" will need to take place in order to translate these longer-term objectives into shorter-term personal targets split into agreed milestones.
- *Non-financial incentives*: A belief that money alone can encourage the enhancement of individual management performance is inaccurate. Other forms of incentive can also include promotion and career development opportunities. The reward system should therefore involve adjustment to issues such as succession planning and career progression or promotion using developmental pathways and career ladders. The chief executive has promised as much for "star performers". This may necessitate a review of the existing structure above SBU level in order to ensure that such positions exist.
- *Consultation with SBU managers, trade union and other relevant groups*: If the revised scheme is to be accepted by SBU managers as appropriate, there needs to be a wide consultation in order that there is universal "buy in".

May 2007 Questions and Answers

May 2007 Questions and Answers

7

Managerial Level

Paper P4 – Organisational Management and Information Systems

The answers published here have been written by the Examiner and should provide a helpful guide for both tutors and students.

Published separately on the CIMA website (www.cimaglobal.com/students) from the end of September 2006 will be a Post Examination Guide for this paper, which will provide much valuable and complementary material including indicative mark information.

CIMA

Business Management Pillar

Managerial Level Paper

P4 – Organisational Management and Information Systems

23 May 2007 – Wednesday Afternoon Session

Instructions to candidates

You are allowed three hours to answer this question paper.
You will be allowed 20 minutes reading time **before the examination begins** during which you should read the question paper and, if you wish, highlight and/or make notes on the question paper. However, you will **not** be allowed, **under any circumstances**, to open the answer book and start writing or use your calculator during this reading time.
You are strongly advised to carefully read ALL the question requirements before attempting the question concerned (that is, all parts and/or sub-questions). The question requirements for Sections B and C are contained in a dotted box.
ALL answers must be written in the answer book. Answers or notes written in the question paper will **not** be submitted for marking.
Answer the ONE compulsory question in Section A. This has fifteen sub-questions on pages 187 to 190.
Answer ALL six compulsory sub-questions in Section B on pages 191 and 192.
Answer ONE of the two questions in Section C on pages 193 and 194.
The list of verbs as published in the syllabus is given for reference at the end of the book.
Write your full candidate number, the paper number and the examination subject title in the spaces provided on the front of the answer book. Also write your contact ID and name in the space provided in the right hand margin and seal to close.
Tick the appropriate boxes on the front of the answer book to indicate which questions you have answered.

SECTION A – 40 MARKS

[the indicative time for answering this section is 72 minutes]

ANSWER *ALL* FIFTEEN SUB-QUESTIONS

Instructions for answering Section A

The answers to the fifteen sub-questions in Section A should ALL be written in your answer book.

Your answers should be clearly numbered with the sub-question number and ruled off so the markers know which sub-question you are answering. **For multiple choice questions you need only write the sub-question number and the answer option you have chosen**. You do not need to start a new page for each sub-question.

Each of the sub-questions numbered from **1.1** to **1.10** inclusive, given below, has only ONE correct answer. Each is worth two marks.

? Question One

1.1 Entity life histories, data flow diagrams and decision tables are all examples of

A requisite variety and system entropy.

B evaluation techniques when appointing a preferred supplier.

C recording techniques used during the analysis and design of a system.

D software considerations in project design.

(2 marks)

1.2 An organisation's credit policy represents a variable within

A the price marketing mix.

B the product marketing mix.

C product placement.

D the matrix of potential sales and growth.

(2 marks)

1.3 According to Porter's value chain, the final primary activity is referred to as

A marketing and sales.

B outbound logistics.

C procurement.

D service.

(2 marks)

1.4 The TQMEX model is a framework that integrates processes associated with

A total quality management experience through accreditation.

B supply chain management.

C both operations and quality management.

D organisational development.

(2 marks)

1.5 Input devices are communication links

A between the user and the computer.

B between hardware and software.

C between processing devices.

D within data processing.

(2 marks)

1.6 In systems theory a sensor is

A the person who acts on "results".

B sensitive personal data used as input.

C the process of being sensitive to (mindful of) the wider environment.

D any device that measures and records the output of a system.

(2 marks)

1.7 Approval of documentation, procedures manuals and work instructions is associated with

A registration under the standards required for quality certification.

B total quality management (TQM).

C lean production methods.

D job evaluation.

(2 marks)

1.8 "Centralised" and "distributed" are examples of

A hard systems approaches to change.

B star networks.

C value chain approaches.

D systems configurations.

(2 marks)

1.9 Rodger's seven-point plan refers to

A quality targets for world class operations.

B implementation guidelines for introducing new hardware.

C the likely headings to be found as part of a person specification.

D lean production processes.

(2 marks)

1.10 The main advantages of a database include

A the development of separate data sources.

B unlimited access and open communication.

C end user flexibility and devolution of responsibility.

D data integrity and elimination of duplication.

(2 marks)

(Total for sub-questions 1.1 to 1.10 = 20 marks)

Requirements

Each of the sub-questions numbered **1.11** to **1.15** below require a brief written response. Each sub-question is worth 4 marks.

Your response should be in note form and must not exceed 50 words per sub-question.

1.11 Explain why a firm might choose **not** to engage in market segmentation after conducting appropriate research.

(4 marks)

1.12 Briefly explain **two** techniques that might be useful in forecasting future market demand for an organisation's products or services.

(4 marks)

1.13 Identify **eight** important documents and information an interviewer should have access to when conducting a job selection interview.

(4 marks)

1.14 Compare and contrast Kaizen and Business Process Re-engineering (BPR).

(4 marks)

1.15 When identifying the requirements of a new system explain what "functional" and "physical" aspects should be taken into account.

(4 marks)

(Total for sub-questions 1.11 to 1.15 = 20 marks)

(Total for Section A = 40 marks)

SECTION B – 30 MARKS

[the indicative time for answering this section is 54 minutes]

ANSWER *ALL* SIX SUB-QUESTIONS. EACH SUB-QUESTION IS WORTH 5 MARKS.

? Question Two

XX is a manufacturing firm with a past reputation for offering a diverse range of innovative products to a traditional market. Three years ago the previous Chief Executive invested in e-commerce as a way of making longer term cost reductions and establishing an advantage over XX's competitors (all of whom trade by more traditional means). A second initiative involved building a carefully designed headquarters (HQ) to cater for a growing central staff needed to control operating activities more tightly. These initiatives were financed by a number of measures including

- the suspension of all other plans for the purchase of computer hardware and software;
- abandoning both training and research and development (R&D) in the short term;
- reducing both marketing and finance budgets;
- suspending all new recruitment even for posts falling vacant.

The Chief Executive explained that

- e-commerce would replace all other forms of trading and both old and new customers would be beating at our door;
- the new HQ would be a visible symbol that "XX means innovation".

Although the new HQ won a prestigious design award, other matters did not go so well and after successive years of financial losses a new Chief Executive was appointed. The new Chief Executive soon recruited a small management team with particular expertise in company analysis and recovery. Its report into XX's problems indicated

- a weakening position relative to competitors due to inappropriate strategies;
- poor management at all levels and a neglect of XX's core business and products;
- weak financial control and management accounting information;
- inappropriate marketing practices and a failure to manage the company's product portfolio leading to unprofitable lines and few new products.

The new Chief Executive indicated several priorities to turnaround the company including

- halting further investment in e-commerce;
- reconsidering budgetary priorities including reducing central costs;
- delayering, decentralisation and re-skilling of the workforce;
- funding the re-establishment of XX's position in the marketplace;
- using software solutions to improve XX's manufacturing operation.

The Chief Executive wishes to present these ideas at the next Board meeting and has asked you to prepare brief notes to support the presentation.

Instructions

Use a separate page of your answer book for each sub-question (meaning that your notes are contained on no more than six pages in total). Your notes can take any form so long as they comply with the page limit and might include diagrams, tables, sentences or bullet points, etc.

Requirements:

Prepare brief notes for the new Chief Executive for each of the sub-questions she has identified below.

(a) Explain how XX can address any **two** of the issues identified by the management team.

(5 marks)

(b) Explain why delayering is more appropriate than downsizing in helping to turnaround XX.

(5 marks)

(c) Explain the disadvantages of using the internet as XX's sole marketing tool.

(5 marks)

(d) Describe the factors that need to be considered by XX when deciding whether to invest in a product.

(5 marks)

(e) Identify the types of software application that would produce most advantage to a manufacturing firm trying to improve its production operations.

(5 marks)

(f) Describe the potential benefits of XX resuming its investment in training.

(5 marks)

(Total for Question Two = 30 marks)

(Total for Section B = 30 marks)

SECTION C – 30 MARKS

[Indicative time for answering this question is 54 minutes]

ANSWER *ONE* QUESTION ONLY

Question Three

YO employs buyers, designers, machinists, tailors and sales people to produce and sell its coats, jackets, trousers, dresses and skirts. YO has a long standing relationship with MX which sells directly to the public from a chain of out of town stores. Over 80% of YO's sales are to MX whose approach has been to sell clothing in great volumes at lower prices than the high street stores. It expects its suppliers (including YO) to take account of new fashion designs and manufacture its clothes at competitive prices.

MX is rethinking its strategy and wishes to move more "upmarket" by introducing a better quality clothing range, which it believes its customers will be prepared to pay a little more for. Already YO has noticed that MX has started to be more demanding by sending back any batches it feels are in the slightest way unsuitable.

MX wants to work with fewer suppliers but develop a better relationship with each of them. MX wants to renegotiate its contract with YO (which expires soon in any case). MX is prepared to talk with YO about the need to improve the quality of its products and has indicated that if it receives the right assurances, it would be prepared to pay a slightly higher unit price per item. It also proposes to work more closely with YO's designers to maximise production of the type of clothing that it feels its customers want.

If these talks are unsuccessful, MX will use one of its other suppliers when the existing contract expires. YO is aware that MX has experimented by using a few trusted overseas suppliers who have managed to achieve both relatively low prices and superior quality through the adoption of total quality management (TQM) techniques.

Anxious to maintain its relationship with MX, YO recognises that it must change from its present focus on price to one that includes quality considerations.

Requirements

(a) Evaluate the way in which MX is proposing to manage its suppliers as part of a value system.

(10 marks)

(b) Discuss the requirements for achieving total quality within YO.

(10 marks)

(c) Describe how YO must change in order to meet MX's new requirements. In your answer you should only consider how YO's human resource practices and the attitude and behaviour of its employees must change.

(10 marks)

(Total for Question Three = 30 marks)

Question Four

ZnZ is a large government funded body that employs several hundred staff performing a wide variety of roles. ZnZ is proud of its commitment to people development and is well known for providing equal opportunities for all its employees. ZnZ employs people regardless of race, religion, gender, sexual orientation or physical disability. The organisation invests heavily in training and development and employs a number of trainees who are studying for their professional examinations. It is left to each professionally qualified member of staff to identify their own training needs and then submit requests for support to their department.

ZnZ's human resource plan is currently being reviewed. As part of this process two significant recommendations have emerged from groups and committees considering future human resource issues.

Recommendation one
(From the HR planning group)
The group has recommended that a more systematic approach to the training and development of qualified staff should be adopted.

Recommendation two
(From the Diversity Committee)
The Committee has recommended that every person who is part of a minority or disadvantaged group should have an individual career coach. Under such a scheme, individuals from these groups would be paired with an experienced colleague on a higher grade who would act as their personal individual career coach. The Committee has issued the following guidelines:

- The scheme will not be associated with the appraisal process.
- Coaches should be approachable, suitably experienced and appropriately trained.
- Coaches will not be the individual's own line manager.
- Regular meetings should take place between the two individuals where they should be able to confidentially discuss any concerns and areas for self-development. Inevitably individuals will wish to discuss career related issues and they should receive appropriate advice from their career coach.

You work for the Director of Human Resourcing who is very sympathetic to the recommendation of the Diversity Committee in particular. (So much so that she feels that the scheme should include all trainees and those middle managers that have been identified as having promotion potential.) She has asked you to investigate both recommendations and brief the management team appropriately.

Requirements

(a) Explain the stages involved in the development for ZnZ of a systematic approach to the training and development of professionally qualified staff.

(10 marks)

(b) Discuss the potential advantages of the individual career coach scheme for ZnZ.

(10 marks)

(c) Discuss the potential disadvantages of the individual career coach scheme for ZnZ.

(10 marks)

(Total for Question Four = 30 marks)

(Total marks for Section C = 30 marks)

The Examiner for OMIS offers to future candidates and to lecturers using this booklet for study purposes, the following background and guidance on the questions included in this examination paper.

Note: This examination paper reflects revised weightings between sections A and C for the first time.

Section A – compulsory

Question one in total accounts for 40% of the paper (previously 50%) and tests topics in all sections of the syllabus apart from Change Management (which is tested in Question two).

Parts 1.1–1.10 tests candidates' knowledge of a wide variety of topics within the syllabus through the use of objective test questions in a conventional "multiple choice" format. (On previous examination diets there were 15 sub questions).

Parts 1.11–1.15 provides further objective testing through limited word responses. These sub questions (valued at 4 marks each) test knowledge and understanding. Sub questions 1.11 and 1.12 test aspects of Marketing, (learning outcome D (ii)), while 1.13 tests learning outcome E (iii) of Managing Human Capital, sub question 1.14 tests Operations Management C(iv), and 1.15 tests Information Systems A (vi) . Responses for each sub question are expected to conform to the word limit indicated of 50 words. Responses beyond this limit are not marked.

Section B – compulsory

Question two represents 30% of the paper and tests topics from Change Management and Marketing, as well as part testing Information Systems and Managing Human Capital. As with previous papers a common workplace related scenario is used from which all sub questions are drawn.
Parts (a) and (b) tests candidates' knowledge and understanding through the application of thinking from Change Management (learning outcome B (iv)). Parts (c) and (d) part test candidates' knowledge and understanding through the application of thinking from Marketing (learning outcome D (v) and (iv)).
Part (e) involves a part testing of learning outcome A(i) (Information systems) and finally part (f) concerns an HR issue associated with E(iii) .
Responses for each sub question are expected on a single side of A4 and in a form that might include diagrams, tables, a few sentences, bullet points, etc. This limit simulates a real life scenario in which accuracy, brevity and clarity are called for and also hopefully prevents candidates from spending a disproportionate amount of time on each sub question.
Responses beyond the limit indicated are not marked.
All sub questions require application of knowledge to the scenario.

Section C – one question from two

Section C accounts for 30% (previously 20%) of the paper and part tests aspects of the syllabus topics of Information Systems, Managing Human Capital and Marketing. Both questions involve the use of business scenarios as contexts. All sub questions require the application of knowledge and understanding to the scenario.

Question three tests candidates' understanding of issues associated with Operations Management (two sub questions) and Managing Human Capital. The question requires an application of knowledge and understanding to the scenario of the relationship of a clothing supplier and a retailer which has decided to move towards more quality orientated products. Sub questions (a) and (b) test C(viii) and C (ix) and sub question (c) tests E(ii). All sub-questions are worth ten marks each.

Question four tests candidates' understanding of issues associated with Managing Human Capital and is set within the context of a large government funded body considering a more systematic approach to the training and development of qualified staff and the introduction of a career coaching scheme. All three sub questions focus on practical aspects of the proposal and in so doing test E(v). All sub-questions are worth ten marks each.

Examiner's Answers

SECTION A

Question One

1.1 C

1.2 A

1.3 D

1.4 C

1.5 A

1.6 D

1.7 A

1.8 D

1.9 C

1.10 D

1.11

- The market is so insubstantial that the effort is not justified
- Market life cycle in decline therefore little future potential
- Difficulty (and cost) in analysing market
- Homogenous market making segmentation unnecessary
- Competitors already established in all profitable segments

1.12

use linked variables

Determine variable. Identify past trends. Project demand accordingly.
Examples:

- DIY retailer: likely home ownership growth
- Ice-cream producer: temperature forecasts

Sales force forecasts

More reliable if sales force is paid commission:

- Ask each region to estimate
- Aggregate figures
- Adjust for over-optimism, etc.

(Note: only two techniques are required. Answers reasonably might have concentrated on quite different techniques such as:

- Buyer survey of intentions
- Expert opinion/judgement
- Statistical techniques using historical sales data
- Market testing of products
- Assessing total market potential/sales and relative market share, etc).

1.13

Organisational
- Job description
- Person specification
- Structure and other detail
- Standard assessment form
- Pay scales
- Policies
- Terms and conditions of service

Individual candidates
- Completed application form
- CV
- References
- Letter of application

(Note: only eight documents/information are required. Answer shows in excess of this to illustrate the potential range. Others not listed here might reasonably be identified also.)

1.14

Both:
- Associated with quality
- Aim for beneficial change and enhanced performance
- Customer-focused
- Involve learning

Kaizen	**BPR**
Continuous improvement	One off exercise
Small incremental steps	Radical changes
Longer term	Short term
Providing workforce with tools and techniques	About business processes and structures and creative use of IT

1.15

"Functional" requirements:
- Each system function (data flow, user needs, etc.)
- Input, output, file (volume, frequency, purpose, etc.)
- Editing, file maintenance controls, backup, etc.

"Physical" requirements:
- Data storage
- Access, updating, growth
- Peripherals and communication
- Processing (centralised, distributed, etc.)
- Outputs, formats
- Screen layouts

SECTION B

Question Two

(a)

(Note: Many of the factors identified by the management team are common with those cited by Slatter as causes of organisational decline. The question only requires a response to two issues, for completeness a fuller answer is provided relating to all the issues.)

Issues

Weakening position relative to competitors due to inappropriate strategies	Refocus on correct strategy • Previous strategy based on differentiation through innovation. But e-commerce introduced to reduce costs. Costs are not significant with a differentiation strategy • Innovation needed in product range not method of trading and new initiatives suggest this may be addressed
Poor management at all levels and a neglect of core business and products	Poor management • New Chief Executive and management team in place • Organisational changes proposed • Counselling, training required • Unsuitable managers released (potential redundancy costs, etc.) Neglect of core business/products • Better management • Performance targets based on core business/products
Weak financial control and management accounting information	• New management team and decentralisation could lead to improved financial control • Reconsidering budgetary priorities could lead to new investment in financial control and management accounting information • Investment needed to design appropriate controls and reports • System implementation issues need addressing • Recruitment of new finance staff • Training required amongst existing finance staff
Inappropriate marketing practices and a failure to manage the company's product portfolio leading to unprofitable lines and few new products	• Reconsidering budgetary priorities could lead to new investment in R & D to develop new lines • Improved management accounting information to identify unprofitable lines • Need to encourage creativity amongst staff for innovation. New performance management and reward systems? • May need to engineer a culture change • New lines need to be market tested • Use consultants to review portfolio, conduct market research, market testing etc.

(b)

Differences between delayering and downsizing:
Delayering and downsizing are both ways of reducing costs through a reduction in the workforce numbers.

Delayering involves:
- removing the "middle layers" of the pyramid of organisational bureaucracies.
- reduction in the number of staff who are not dealing directly with external customers.
- shortening the span of command, speeding decision-making and getting the organisation "closer to its customer".

Downsizing involves:
- refocusing by removing business activities that are 'non-core' or non profitable.
- creating smaller more flexible, fast-moving, efficient and viable local business units.

Reason why delayering is appropriate to XX:
The purpose-built headquarters (HQ) is meant to cater for "a growing central staff" needed to control activities more tightly.

However, these staff have not been effective, as evidenced by
- poor management.
- a neglect of XX's core business and products.
- weak financial control.

As part of delayering these central staff would presumably be eliminated. This in turn would empower the lower levels of the organisational pyramid to exercise control locally. Hopefully delayering (in particular) might also lead to more efficient operations.

(c)

Disadvantages of using the internet alone as a marketing device:
Loss of potential business
- Design of user-friendly protocols and screen designs a new challenge. The design of pages must be carefully considered and developed to achieve maximum impact. XX may not have the necessary skills and the use of a web designer may have to be commissioned.
- May lose some existing customers to those competitors who do not use this technology, so weakening customer loyalty.
- XX's site must be secure and be seen to be secure. Site security concerns could deter potential business.

Exclusion of vital market segment
- Only part of the market is accessed (i.e. those with computerised operations and prepared to do business on-line). The technology might deny access to certain suppliers for similar reason.

Negative image projection
- Presents a certain image (distant, virtual, impersonal, etc.) that may be unattractive, particularly to local or traditional customer base.

Demands of the technology
- Need for sophisticated support systems.
- Training and re-skilling costs.
- Need to maintain, implying potentially the need to employ a web master.
- Investment in software architecture (e.g. linking back-office stock inventories to front-office transactions software).

All involve cost.

(d)

Factors that need to be considered by XX when deciding whether to invest in a product:

Demand

- The degree of growth in the market for the product. According to the product life cycle, products pass through distinct stages. The cycle can be used to help determine appropriate strategies for the firm and help make decisions over investment in products. A product at introduction or growth stage is worthy of investment, maturity and decline, not so.
- "Postponability" of the product to the purchaser. The greater the postponability the greater the temptation to invest in promotional campaigns.
- Activities of direct competitors and whether product investment will spark self-defeating retaliatory action by competitors.
- The policy of competitors in investing in new products/existing products.

Economic

- The potential revenue streams from the product.
- The product's profitability levels.
- Size of investment required, XX's funds available and ability to invest effectively/ appropriately in the product.

Risk

- Market reaction (through research) to the product.
- Risk associated with product whether social or political sensitivities or level of financial costs that may not be recovered.

Internal relationships

- The value of the product to the overall portfolio. The product may be key to all other products in the entire portfolio.
- The demands and priorities suggested by other products within the portfolio.

(e)

Software applications

There are several distinct types of applications that could be introduced including:
Computer aided design (CAD) and computer aided/automated manufacturing (CAM).
Advantages:

- Long term cost reduction

(f)

The benefits of XX investing in training once more:
Positive impact on workforce:

- Training can lead to increased morale and increased feelings of commitment
- Seen as part of career development
- Seen as part of the reward and remuneration package
- Signals a new (enlightened) era in the company's history

Strategic HR considerations:

- Fill skill gaps: non-recruitment policy suggests that there must be such gaps. If left unfilled XX will grow increasingly ineffective
- Training can be a more cost effective way of filling essential skill gaps rather than using contractors or recruiting additional staff with those skills
- Ethically appropriate as it represents an investment in the human resource
- Enhances shared skills and helps workforce flexibility

Contribution to turnaround of the company through appropriate well-designed training:

- Potentially improves efficiency of operation
- Potentially improves competitiveness, particularly if competitors are not investing to the same degree

SECTION C

The answers that follow are fuller and more comprehensive than would have been expected from a well-prepared candidate. They have been written in this way to aid teaching, study and revision for tutors and candidates alike.

Question Three

(a)

Most products arise through several organisations combining and trading with one another from sourcing raw materials, to design, development, manufacture and then bringing the final product to market. In these circumstances relationships between several organisations combine to create a value network comprising of a series of value chains.

Both MX and YO form part of a wider value network with YO undertaking the design and manufacture stages. In this example YO represents the supplier value chain whilst MX's own value chain interacts with the final customer. (YO presumably also has a supplier or suppliers of cloth that it makes designs for and then manufactures clothing from). Michael Porter's work in this area stresses the need for good management of the value network in order to gain competitive advantage and "create and sustain superior performance".

In Porter's terms relationships between the firms in the value system matter. The overall value system describes the position of a firm relative to the firms upstream and downstream of it:

- MX is upstream (nearer the ultimate customer) of YO
- YO along with MX's other suppliers are downstream of MX
- YO's suppliers of cloth are downstream of YO

When viewing supply strategically the nature of relationships with suppliers becomes key. When relationships are based on driving down price they can be quite adversarial. Alternatively, more collaborative arrangements operate where there is a joint quest to reduce costs and a sharing of technology and innovations (known as 'partnership sourcing').

The way an organisation manages its supply process is known as its "sourcing strategies" and the success of these clearly has strategic implications. MX in the past appeared to favour a traditional strategy known as the "multiple" option. Here MX as the buyer chooses several sources of supply (both home and abroad). Individual suppliers under this arrangement become less powerful and prices can be driven down as a result. It is fairly obvious that YO is far more dependent upon MX (as its number one customer with 80% of its sales) than MX is on YO. MX seems to have realised however that this may not be necessarily conducive to good working relationships. Meaningful supplier relationships and reliance on trusted suppliers is necessary in order to achieve a quality product. In the past MX has relied on low prices in order to make sales but now it is rethinking its strategy and wishes to move more "up market" by introducing a better quality clothing range, which it believes its customers will be prepared to pay a little more for. MX proposes to work more closely with YO's designers to maximise production of the type of clothing that it feels its customers want. Both organisations have a long-standing relationship with one another, and assuming that YO is prepared to change its approach to one more akin to TQM it will become one of MX's preferred suppliers. This means that with fewer suppliers MX will be able to concentrate on developing their relationship more fully.

Consistent with Porter's thinking both MX and YO as firms in the value system now have an opportunity to collaborate more fully in order to increase total value (by increasing the ability of the final product to generate maximum customer satisfaction). In this case it will be through making a better quality product including taking more care to ensure that the design is "right" (appropriate). Competitive advantage through linkages between the organisation and its value system components is being attempted in this case by applying TQM (total quality management) principles.

(b)

The underlying concepts of quality
Organisations that compete on the basis of price must ensure low-cost operations in order to be successful. Cost containment in material sourcing, production, and distribution is important. Resultant cost savings from these activities can (in part) be passed on to their customers. These organisations believe that their customers value the relatively low cost of the product (commensurate with a certain level of quality). By comparison, a company competing on the basis of quality will try to achieve a better quality product that will appeal to less price-sensitive consumers. In these circumstances quality rather than price will be the key consideration in bringing goods to the market. It is apparent that MX is altering its view of what it believes its customers value most (namely improved quality rather than low cost). This is unsurprising, as quality is increasingly being recognised as a critical issue for modern organisations operating in sometimes hostile environments with intense competition and demanding customers.

MX is said to want to move more "up market" by introducing an altogether better quality clothing range. This change in strategy will require less of an emphasis on price in favour of approaches that achieve quality. The need to satisfy customers' needs is central to most understandings of quality. Quality should in fact be best understood from the perspective of the customer, including their expectations and specific requirements. MX is by far YO's biggest customer with in excess of 80% of total sales and has made its requirements quite clearly. Given its dependence on MX, YO has little option but to adopt a quality approach in order to satisfy its major customer.

'Total quality'
There are many definitions of quality. Quality guru Philip P Crosby is known for his emphasis on achieving Zero Defects (no faulty products) and maintaining that *Quality is Free*. He explained quality as meaning getting everyone to deliver what he or she has agreed and *getting it right the first time*.

There are a number of approaches to ensuring total quality, most popularly Total Quality Management (TQM). MX's overseas suppliers apparently are able to achieve relatively low prices and superior quality through the adoption of TQM. This involves developing an organisational culture founded on a belief in quality so that:

- Everyone (including customers and suppliers) is involved in this continuous process.
- The quality requirements of customers are central.
- There is the full commitment of senior management.

Key quality concepts
There are certain fundamental concepts that any organisation wishing to establish a quality ethos must adhere to including:

- *Commitment from the top.* If management is not fully committed, it is unlikely that customer requirements of quality will be met. (In YO's case the commitment is obvious: M is its most significant customer and it must change in order to survive at its present level of operation).
- *Competence.* Quality is achieved through competence in whatever activity is undertaken. Competence can only be gained through continuous training, skill development and experience. YO needs to commit funds to training, recruitment and people development, etc.
- *Communication.* The importance of quality must be effectively communicated throughout the organisation in order to improve understanding of its purpose and benefits. YO needs to develop a communication strategy that includes briefings, written reminders and visible symbols. The key message for YO is to change practice in order to retain its most important customer: MX.

- *Continuous improvement.* The *Kaizen* philosophy will involve the continual analysis of processes to allow continued improvement in performance and quality. YO will need to develop a non-threatening culture, possibly involving quality circles and training facilitators to ensure that this takes place.

(c)

Employee Groups
MX has indicated that if it receives the right assurances on quality it would be prepared to pay YO a higher unit cost per product. Although the idea of cost containment cannot be abandoned altogether YO's staff will be required to think and act in different ways, and most importantly with a greater regard for quality.

The following might be the new considerations for different groups:

- **Buyers** should now concentrate on purchasing better quality cloth: not the cheapest available. Buyers should therefore be given new targets and a revised purchasing criterion.
- **Fashion designers** should now seek to create an attractive clothing range that will be seen by the buyer as being of a higher quality. This may involve practices that call for more originality than simply copying top fashion designs. This may involve the need to recruit new staff with these different skills. Clearly the need to work collaboratively alongside MX's own designers will be key.
- Clothing **machinists and tailors** should now concentrate on getting it 'right first time' rather than aiming to produce as many items as possible. This will involve them in self-checking their own work and operating to new performance measures.
- The **sales force** should appreciate that the nature of the products is now different. This might involve them finding new customers for the 20% of production that will not be taken up by MX. These new customers should be prepared to pay a little more for the product but will demand better quality, and a more demanding after-sales service. (It is impractical for 80% of the production to be quality orientated and 20% cost orientated).

HR practices
By moving away from cost to quality as a focus there will be many human resource (HR) considerations. These will involve the development of new policies and practices. All these changes will require adjustments to HR practices as follows:

- The introduction of staff **training** to educate staff of the imperative of quality and the development of specific work related competences that will be needed to improve quality.
- A different emphasis will need to be applied in YO's **recruitment** practices. This might involve offering higher pay in exchange for higher quality work. It may be a good idea to attract new staff that have come from organisations that operate TQM.
- YO should pay particular attention to the **retention** of workers who produce consistently high quality work and seem to embrace the TQM philosophy. New **employment packages** may need to be considered.
- In terms of **rewards** YO will need to introduce revised performance measures and bonuses to encourage quality rather than the maximisation of outputs.
- **Cultural re-engineering** will be needed to achieve continuous improvement, and HR can play an important role.
- **Reporting** mechanisms will need to be readjusted (including HR) so as to emphasise the monitoring of quality more than the monitoring of cost.

These practices can then be translated into achieving:

- *Commitment* (Staff training for understanding and buy-in, and performance measurement and rewards to reinforce the message).
- *Competence* (Staff training for new skills and attitudes. Continual training and development of skills and experience in quality achievement. Selection and retention policy to attract and keep the "right" people).

- *Communication* (Staff training to "sell" quality throughout all levels of YO).
- *Continuous improvement* (This philosophy requires that the organisational culture will need to be re-engineered and training available in quality circles and TQM practices).

? Question Four

(a)

Establish responsibility for the process
In order that a systematic approach is adopted, then a process should be developed and led by Human Resourcing. They should be accountable to ZnZ executive for the successful delivery of training and development for this group. It is likely that ZnZ is organised into departments or divisions and these should be involved throughout.

A more systematic approach to the training and development of qualified staff might involve the following stages (or similar):

Establishing a baseline
From what information is available the following is known (or can reasonably be guessed at):

- ZnZ invests heavily in training and development and employs a number of trainees who are studying for their professional examinations. Dependent upon staff turnover rates and retention of this group of employees, it is reasonable to assume that qualified staff might represent a substantial number.
- ZnZ employs several hundred staff performing a wide variety of roles, implying that there are a number of professional groups to be catered for.
- The HR planning group has not indicated that the resource directed to the training and development of qualified staff is too little, more that it could be more systematically applied. It may be that different professional groups are being dealt with in different ways.

As part of establishing the present position, Human Resourcing should identify the numbers of staff involved, the professional groupings they belong to and the level of training and development they have received to date.

Training and development: Professional requirement
Most professional bodies (including CIMA) require their members to engage in continuing professional development (CPD) in order that the currency of their members' skill and knowledge is maintained. This requirement should be readily available for each group involved by reference to the professional bodies/the departments concerned.

Training and development: Organisational requirement
Functional plans (such as the HR plan) should be consistent with and support the overall corporate plan or strategy. An assessment should be made of the knowledge, skills and competencies required of the workforce in order to deliver ZnZ's strategy successfully. This will undoubtedly imply management and other business skills that qualified staff will require.

Training and development: personal requirement
A training needs analysis (or similar) could be conducted whereby the existing skills and competencies of an individual are mapped against the organisational and professional needs and an individual training plan developed. Similarly, training needs identified as part of the appraisal processes might usefully be collated. The outcome of this process could then be discussed and agreed with departments.

Establish options for training and development provision
The next stage is to identify the most appropriate means of filling the training and development gaps identified. Attention should be given to the following main considerations:

- Feasible delivery methods (such as classroom delivery, distance learning, on the job training, technology supported learning, etc. or some blended combination).
- In-house provision or external provision. ZnZ may already have in place trainers who are part of the payroll and/or specialist providers and consultants who have successfully worked on its behalf in the past.
- Onsite or offsite provision. There are advantages and disadvantages of each and it may be that a mixed approach rather than either/or might be adopted. Provision onsite would require adequate training facilities to be available to ZnZ.
- Availability of externally provided support and courses. Rather than a bespoke provision, it may be sufficient to meet some individuals needs by sending them to some other commercial provider or educational or professional establishments.

It would be a good idea to liaise with departments and professional staff when making decisions over the options available.

Costing of options and agreement of a budget
The financial cost should be calculated, as should other resource commitments, including the number of days release required from work. These should be presented to ZnZ's management and approved as appropriate.

Feedback and means of measuring effectiveness of training and development provision
This should include the establishment of criteria for provision and the establishment of measures and performance indicators. With this information, monitoring can take place and improvements brought about.

It is also important that regular structured feedback should be received from qualified staff, both as individuals and as small focus groups.

(b)

The proposed scheme, if properly introduced, has several potential advantages and when operated should be capable of performing a positive role within the organisation at a number of levels. Specifically, it should help to:

Strengthen the existing culture
ZnZ is likely to have a distinctive culture that could be further strengthened by the proposals. The organisation may be diverse in its operations but it is distinctive due to the fact that it is a public sector body and it has (an apparently) caring, people orientated culture. The scheme should fulfil the role of reinforcing the organisation's commitment to people development and provide confirmation in deed as well as word. The fact that it is a genuine equal opportunity employer is evidenced by its attention to diversity, and support for minority and disadvantaged groups through effective career coaching.

Lead to Organisational Development
The scheme might be viewed as an example of best practice and a demonstration of a considerate attitude by the organisation, so reinforcing the overall culture.

The scheme may also strengthen organisational communication, positively contribute to knowledge sharing and erode departmentalism (a commitment to one's department rather than the organisation more widely) particularly if participants and coaches are from different working areas. (There is no suggestion of departmentalism from the scenario but this is often the case in large diverse organisations.).

Support HR initiatives
Career coaching can assist current HR initiatives and strategies in the following ways:

- By enhancing a total employment package offered to potential and existing employees. This should make both recruitment and retention less problematic. Dedicated individual support through career coaching might be viewed as an additional valued part of the employment package and an incentive for those groups who may feel alienation (the disadvantaged, the minority groups, those studying and under pressure middle managers).
- By offering new training and challenges for career coaches who are involved in the process. This might lead to greater personal development, motivation and job enrichment.
- The scheme will certainly increase the effectiveness of ZnZ's heavy investment in training and development, particularly for trainees.
- The scheme might be viewed by the organisation as a way of maintaining harmonious relationships in the workplace so avoiding damaging and confrontational industrial relation tensions.

ZnZ's future human resource plan is currently being reviewed and career coaching should enhance future provision.

Supporting key groups
The Diversity Committee has recommended that the scheme should be introduced for minority and disadvantaged groups and the Director of Human Resourcing has expanded the suggestion to include all trainees and those middle managers that have been identified as having promotion potential. All these are key groups within the organisation who should now feel better supported by the proposal.

In particular, **vulnerable groups** will feel more valued and less marginalised. The scheme should help avoid organisational discrimination (which is undesirable and possibly illegal). It should also avoid the isolation of disadvantaged groups. **Trainees** studying for their professional examinations should feel encouraged knowing that "help is at hand". **Middle managers** that have been identified as having promotion potential are a group who require nurturing as part of a career development plan. It would be counter productive if this group were to feel isolated or disaffected and leave. Coaching should help them.

Organisational behaviour is shaped by the so-called "psychological contract" (an unwritten series of mutual expectations of rights, privileges, duties and obligations). It involves a process of giving and receiving by both the organisation and the individual. For instance, the individual might expect of the organisation a decent, clean working environment, respect of the individual and recognition of contribution and achievement. In return, the organisation might expect of the individual a respect of authority, fellow workers, customers and suppliers, and a degree of loyalty. The mentoring scheme might be viewed by the individual as a way of valuing the individual and seeking ways of overcoming difficulties that make work difficult or unpleasant. As such, it should strengthen the psychological contract.

The cost advantages of the scheme
The scheme might be seen as cost effective in that it will

- increase the effectiveness of expenditure on professional training (hopefully, fewer trainees will fail their professional examinations).
- potentially increase job satisfaction, motivation and feelings of commitment which will be reflected in better job performance and hence greater productivity levels.
- Support minority, disadvantaged groups, trainees and some middle managers which will hopefully lead to less staff turnover negating the need to undertake expensive recruitment of replacement staff.

(c)

Undeniably, there are potential advantages associated with the proposals. There may also be certain disadvantages, some of which are identified as follows:

Provoking unrest and hostility towards the scheme
There may be individuals and groups however, who do not share the same enthusiasm shown by the Diversity Committee and the Director of Human Resourcing. Indeed, rather than displaying apathy, for some there may be hostility to the scheme.

Some may be cynical about the scheme's motives, others may believe that it is an example of tokenism and more should be done for these groups.

For the uncommitted, the potential benefits of the scheme will need to be communicated and the proposals positively "sold". There will be a need to respond to negative attitudes and real concerns with practical solutions that can be incorporated into the scheme design.

Making excluded groups feel that they are disadvantaged
The scheme could be attacked for being elitist and selective. Currently, the scheme is to extend to

- minority groups (however defined).
- disadvantaged groups (however defined).
- all trainees.
- middle managers that have been identified as having promotion potential.

For those groups that are not offered the same facility, there may be some resentment and loss of motivation. The following groups will not be (apparently) eligible:

- Newly qualified professionals
- First line managers
- Senior managers
- Middle managers who have been identified as having no promotion potential

For the latter group, this may be very demotivating, particularly if the group is identified for the first time. They may also feel stigmatised if they see their contemporaries benefiting from career coaching.

HR will need to consider either the potential benefits of expanding the scheme still more widely or considering how they might best support those groups excluded by the scheme.

Potential for undermining line managers
Line managers of participants may feel that the process could undermine their authority or position. Clear guidelines as to the extent of their duties will need to be issued to coaches to overcome this potential difficulty.

Costs of setting up the scheme
There will be a number of practical difficulties associated with the proposal, initially involving setting up the scheme and then operating and maintaining it. The scheme will require careful investigation of best practice elsewhere, planning and communication as well as engaging a wide number of stakeholders in establishing the scheme.

Appropriate training for mentors will need to be organised which has cost and scheduling implications.

Costs of running the scheme
Once operational, certain participants may be too demanding of their coaches in terms of (possibly unreasonable) expectation, demands and time. Ways of overcoming these difficulties will need to be devised.

The scheme will not be cost neutral, as coaches will all be experienced and on a higher grade. Their time therefore, will involve an opportunity cost (as there is a need for regular meetings). For the coach, this might translate into making their working lives more stressful and lead them to be less effective in their day to day working. This issue will need to be considered by HR.

Other practical issues may arise from the operation of the scheme including:

- The position of trainees. Should they also be allowed to continue being coached once they have passed their examinations?
- Coaches who leave the organisation or do not fulfil their obligations correctly.

Finding measures to judge the success of the scheme
There will be a need to review the effectiveness of the scheme after it has operated for a while. It would be helpful therefore, to establish appropriate criteria and performance indicators before the scheme commences and these can be used as measures of effectiveness as part of such a review. Such indicators of performance may be difficult to arrive at and agree upon.